The Art of Lean Filmmaking

An unconventional guide
to creating independent feature films

Kylie Eddy & David Eddy

First published by Lean Filmmaking in 2021.

Copyright © 2021 Kylie Eddy and David Eddy. All rights reserved.

Feel free to take passages from this book and replicate them online or in print, but link back to leanfilmmaking.com. If you want to use more than a few paragraphs, email book@leanfilmmaking.com.

A catalogue record of this book is available from the National Library of Australia.

Editor: Irene Kalpakas
Cover Design: The Who Photography & Design

ISBN: 9780645200706 (paperback)
ISBN: 9780645200713 (ebook)

leanfilmmaking.com

Disclaimer: the information in this book is designed to provide helpful guidance on the subjects discussed and isn't a substitute for professional financial, legal, occupational health and safety or any other advice. The authors disclaim any liability to any person arising directly or indirectly from the use of, or for any errors in or omissions from, the information contained in this book. The adoption and application of the information in this book is at the reader's discretion and is their sole responsibility.

Contents

Introduction: A new way to make films with creativity at its heart   1

Part 1: Core Values

The Lean Filmmaking Philosophy   17
Collaboration is key   19
Fan focused first   22
Story before production values   24
Learn by doing   27
Make-Show-Adjust Cycles   29
Values can transform creativity   33
What you need to start (and it isn't money)   34

Part 2: Step by Step Guide

The Lean Filmmaking Method   39

Step 1: Form Squad   47
Start with a squad, not a script   50
Recruit for skills, not roles   51
Choose the minimum viable squad   54
Align squad goals   58
A squad needs transparency and moxie   64
You're done with this step when…   74

Step 2: Discover Fans   77
Let's talk about talking to fans   82
Start with a spark   90

Conduct research interviews	92
Draft a fan experience	103
Make tester videos	104
You're done with this step when...	116
Step 3: Develop Drafts	**119**
Ceremonies empower the squad	122
Restructure work by overlapping activities	124
Delay decisions with just-in-time production	127
Construct the Story Scaffold	129
Run full-film draft Make-Show-Adjust Cycles	139
You're done with this step when...	157
Step 4: Produce Polishes	**161**
Ask fans to pay for it	166
Scale the squad (but only if you really need to)	168
Prioritize with the Impact-vs-Difficulty Matrix	170
Run full-film polish Make-Show-Adjust Cycles	172
You're done with this step when...	183
Step 5: Launch Film	**187**
Stop obsessing about film festivals	191
Demystify self-distribution	195
Run marketing and sales experiments	207
Release the film	209
It's out, now what?	212
You're really done when...	213
Conclusion	215
Glossary	216
About Lean Filmmaking	224
Acknowledgments	225

Introduction: A new way to make films with creativity at its heart

It's hard to make an independent feature film.

You need to plan everything down to the last detail, have all the right gear and be able to deliver high production values on a low budget. You've worked on your passion project for years: writing the script, pitching to producers, networking with talent, all while juggling family, friends and probably a full-time job.

You've only got one chance to make your first feature film so it's got to be perfect.

Your reputation, life savings and future career are all on the line.

Fuck that.

Conventional filmmaking methods not only hinder creativity but also waste massive amounts of time, money and energy, often on things that aren't important to an audience.

In the last few decades, technology has dramatically changed filmmaking. The end-to-end production process has been compressed, equipment is more affordable than ever and online distribution gives filmmakers direct access to audiences.

But despite this rapid progress in technology, filmmaking is still an inherently risky business filled with uncertainty.

Lean Filmmaking is the result of more than five years spent experimenting, testing and re-imagining a new way to make films with creativity at its heart.

We began questioning traditional filmmaking models after producing our own independent feature film. The entire process felt grueling, frustrating and demoralizing.

We wanted to find another way.

Inspired by lean manufacturing, lean startups, design thinking and agile software development, we challenged ourselves to look at every aspect of filmmaking from a fresh perspective.

We also reached out to other filmmakers to see if they struggled with the same issues.

Turns out we weren't alone.

We ran meetups to test ideas and got feedback from actors, writers, directors, cinematographers, editors, producers and creatives from all walks of life. We talked to thousands of filmmakers and conducted over sixty one-on-one interviews.

Based on this research we developed some surprising, often counterintuitive, strategies to dramatically improve the filmmaking process, including:
- Collaborating in non-hierarchical, cross-functional squads
- Working in ongoing iterative Make-Show-Adjust Cycles
- Validating assumptions with early fan feedback

We've distilled what we've learned so far into this book so you can put it into action too.

A little bit about us

We're Kylie Eddy (a writer, director and producer) and David Eddy (a software developer and agile coach).

Yup, we're also siblings.

We've combined our skills to create Lean Filmmaking.

Our goal is to provide an alternative pathway for filmmakers to make their independent feature films and build sustainable creative careers.

We want to lower the barriers of entry so filmmaking is accessible to everyone, especially for those people who are underrepresented in the industry, and encourage more diverse storytelling on screen.

We began applying lean and agile principles to the development, production, marketing and distribution of films in 2011. What started as a small experiment grew into the largest filmmaking Meetup group in Australia at the time, with over 2,700 members.

Since then we've produced over fifty events that include everything from filmmaking workshops where everyone makes a short video in an hour, through to an accelerator program with squads who developed micro-budget feature films in fifteen weeks.

The film that sparked Lean Filmmaking

In 2007, Kylie wrote, directed and produced a micro-budget independent feature film for $22,000.

It almost killed her.

Despite doing everything right by traditional filmmaking standards, her film failed.

Before attempting to make a feature film, she spent years studying media and screenwriting at university, worked in marketing for a major distributor (and managed a video store when that was still a thing), went to every seminar and read all the books. She'd also written and directed a couple of successful short films.

Despite all of this, she spent four years trying to get her debut feature film funded.

Kylie wrote many, many drafts of the script, submitted it for grants, hawked it to experienced producers, and networked her ass off. All of this was around her day job, because obviously she still had to pay the rent.

Finally she raised the money herself through private investment from some very generous individual supporters (before crowdfunding existed).

She did this during four months of pre-production.

The film was shot in rural Australia over thirteen days with two actors and a crew of eleven.

Then she spent four months in hellish post-production.

After years of hard slog, the film played at some well-regarded niche international festivals and had a limited DVD release in North America.

Before disappearing into obscurity.

It never made a cent.

While it was an incredible learning experience and massive personal achievement, Kylie was broken – physically, emotionally and financially.

After working towards this dream for over fifteen years, now that it was done she never wanted to make a film again.

Around the same time, David was managing an agile team to develop software and was already seeing the benefits of working in this new way. After listening to his sister's struggles, he realized the process of making films was much like the old waterfall model of software development.

David thought it would be interesting to try an experiment: apply agile principles to filmmaking.

Kylie thought this sounded like bullshit.

After years of investing in traditional filmmaking theory, there was so much to unlearn – but with David's expertise in agile coaching, and relentless optimism that it could work, she gradually came around.

Especially when she started seeing results that were impossible
to ignore.

At the beginning we started small.

In the first instance we asked, will ten filmmakers attend an event about this concept we called Lean Filmmaking?

Yes, they would.

Are they interested enough to come back and maybe bring a friend?

Honestly, most people thought we were deluded! But a small passionate group emerged and they wanted more.

Then it snowballed into hosting fortnightly meetups to test our new ideas.

After several months of theoretical debates, we were ready for a practical experiment.

We produced the Filmmakathon, loosely based on the structure of a tech hackathon, specifically designed for filmmakers to learn about Lean Filmmaking. Over a weekend, two squads each made a short film. That's from nothing to done, all while working with new people, receiving feedback and screening the finished film in front of a live audience.

There was no script, no advance pre-production and no budget.

Everyone had to work within their constraints: using only the actors in their squads, shooting with gear they already owned, keeping locations within walking distance, and of course the biggest constraint – time.

It was an explosion of creativity.

We blasted through stumbling blocks.

We solved problems in a collaborative way.

One of the participants called it an "enthusiasm engine".

This was the confidence boost we needed. We knew this was the right direction.

We'll talk more about this first Filmmakathon experiment in Part 1: Core Values.

Then we wanted to test our next hypothesis: can we make feature films using the Lean Filmmaking method?

For this experiment, we created an Independent Feature Film Accelerator with two squads who developed micro-budget features in fifteen weeks, around day jobs. It was designed for filmmakers who'd already produced short-form content and were looking to take the leap into their first feature films.

We coached the squads through the method, taking high-level concepts through to full-length draft versions of their feature films. Along the way they tackled audience discovery, made concept videos and built momentum for their projects.

We were all astounded at how much was achieved in such a short time.

"It was the kick up the backside we needed. The accelerator was both inspiring and, in a more practical sense, essential to making our debut feature film." —Perri Cummings and Paul Anthony Nelson, producers *Trench*

"The accelerator gave us all the optimism of pre-production without the doom and gloom of post-production." —Melanie Rowland, producer *Time Apart*

We'll talk more about this Independent Feature Film Accelerator in Part 2: Step by Step Guide.

It's been so rewarding to use the tough lessons learned from Kylie's first feature film to create something new and positive. If she hadn't failed, it's unlikely we would've taken drastic action to completely re-imagine the filmmaking process.

How this book works

The Lean Filmmaking method can be used to make any kind of content, but in this book we specifically focus on independent feature films.

Through our experiments, we've also realized that traditional film terminology comes with a lot of baggage. We've come up with some new terms that are explained as we go (and there's a full list of definitions in the glossary).

This book is divided into two parts.

Part 1: Core Values
The philosophy of Lean Filmmaking and how the four core values work together with Make-Show-Adjust Cycles to transform the filmmaking process.

Part 2: Step by Step Guide
A detailed guide to the five-step Lean Filmmaking method, from the idea to the launch of an independent feature film.

This book will work best for those with a solid understanding of filmmaking fundamentals. It doesn't include information about film basics like how to write, shoot, direct, act or edit.

It's ideal for filmmakers who already have experience making short films, series or online videos, and want to transition into making a feature film.

Lean doesn't mean cheap

Before we get into the guts of this book, there's a common misconception that's important to dispel.

Lean doesn't mean cheap or low budget.

When we talk about lean, we're referring to the broader ideology that is used in industries like manufacturing, software development or startups. In this context, it's a set of principles that focus on providing a high value for customers with the least amount of waste.

Being cost-effective is one way to be lean, although that's really just the beginning.

A lack of timely communication, an unproductive team structure or a misunderstanding of audience expectations can undermine the success of a film as much as the budget. But inefficiencies in the filmmaking process are rarely interrogated and often even invisible because "that's how it's always been done".

When applying lean principles to filmmaking, we've purposely weeded out wasteful practices, focused on providing value to audiences and found unique ways to save money, time and energy.

Get ready to be brave

Conventional ideas about how to make an independent feature film simply don't hold true anymore.

At the very least they can be treated with healthy skepticism.

Many of the things you've been told that you *must* do are not required.

These include:
- × Writing a perfect script
- × Raising lots of money before production
- × Pitching to industry professionals
- × Planning everything in advance

But there are other things that are normally postponed to the end of the filmmaking process, or ignored completely, that you'll need to do instead.

These include:
- × Forming a small creative squad
- × Talking to fans early and often
- × Working within constraints
- × Embracing the motto "Done is better than perfect"

In the beginning, the Lean Filmmaking method seems unconventional because it's all new.

It turns traditional notions upside down, shakes up the status quo and encourages courageous conversations about the nature of work.

But the radical will soon become routine.

"If you have a background in production, Lean Filmmaking goes against every instinct you've ever been taught. I spent a long time resisting it but in the end, I was convinced. It changes the way you think about how to make your film." —Melanie Rowland, producer *Time Apart*

"Lean Filmmaking is nothing less than revolutionary for those looking to launch themselves as screen artists, to find a way to channel their voice into a viable, affordable feature film project with results as close to instantaneous as this business gets."
—Perri Cummings and Paul Anthony Nelson, producers *Trench*

Embrace the Lean Filmmaking philosophy and practice the five-step method to make your own independent feature film a reality too.

Let's make films happen together!

Part 1:
Core Values

The Lean Filmmaking Philosophy

We're standing in front of twelve daring filmmakers.

The nervous energy is palpable.

No one knows what to expect.

After months of hypotheticals, we're finally putting Lean Filmmaking into practice for the first time.

Can we really make films using our method?

We'd designed the Filmmakathon (our version of a tech hackathon for filmmakers) to make short films in a weekend using iterative cycles. We'd start from scratch on Friday night, work all Saturday, then on Sunday afternoon screen whatever was made to a live audience.

There was no script, no advance pre-production and no budget. None of the participants had even worked together as teams before now.

We were hoping for paradigm shifts, exponential learning

and major breakthroughs (and we expected some intense meltdowns too).

All of that happened – but it also helped to crystallize our ideas about this new way of making films, test the core values and solidify the definition of Lean Filmmaking.

Lean Filmmaking is a new way of making films with creativity at its heart that enhances collaboration, uses ongoing iterative cycles and forges a deep connection between filmmakers and their fans.

The Lean Filmmaking philosophy has four core values:
- × Collaboration is key
- × Fan focused first
- × Story before production values
- × Learn by doing

The core values remain relevant even as technology improves, storytelling techniques change and shiny new gadgets are invented. They are applicable regardless of genre or format, documentary or narrative, episodic series or feature film.

The core values are reassuring touchstones to help get you unstuck, provide direction and give clarity.

Understanding the core values of the Lean Filmmaking philosophy empowers you to take ownership of the method and integrate it into your creative practice.

Let's take a look at the values in detail and see how they truly transform the way films can be made when combined with Make-Show-Adjust Cycles.

Collaboration is key

We prioritize working together in ways that strengthen meaningful collaboration.

This is achieved by operating in small squads that are cross-functional, non-hierarchical and self-organizing, with everyone sharing responsibility for delivering the film.

The benefits of working collaboratively include:
- Improving communication and increasing transparency
- Using overlapping activities to maximize output
- Quickly adapting to avoid costly delays
- Finding and solving problems early
- Enhancing squad members' potential (and opportunities to learn more skills)

We use the term squad rather than cast and crew (or even team). It's more inclusive of all the skills required to create a film and suggests a different style of working together.

Squad
A group of three to nine multi-skilled people with the combined experience to make a film, including writing, directing, acting, editing, shooting, producing and marketing. Everyone is involved for the duration of making the film, from development to distribution. The overarching purpose of each squad member is to successfully deliver a film to fans, not just execute their specific role.

Collaboration is enhanced by having a cross-functional squad with all members having multiple skills, for example writing/acting/producing or directing/shooting/editing.

It's useful to think about the range of skills needed rather than formal job titles. This allows other valuable skills to be included in the mix like audience development, marketing and Lean Filmmaking coaching.

Being a generalist, rather than a specialist, is an advantage.

To keep squads small, everyone is expected to jump in when required, performing tasks not normally in their job description, like holding a boom mic, conducting audience interviews or carrying gear.

And we're not kidding when we say that all squad members are involved throughout the entire process of making the film.

Actors and editors are in the squad from the very beginning and writers are there right until the end. This one change radically affects many elements of filmmaking that are taken for granted.

The structure of the squad is non-hierarchical. The director isn't in charge in the traditional sense; they're more of a "servant leader". Squad members have shared power in decision-making.

This doesn't mean it's filmmaking by committee.

Rather, it's a much more rigorous way for each squad member to be responsible for their contribution to the project. Creative decisions are made by all squad members based on what's best for the whole film, not just one department.

Developing all aspects of the film together builds trust, provides transparency and highlights areas for workflow improvements.

Because the squads are small, problems are detected earlier, communication is simpler and it's easier to quickly adapt to changing circumstances.

As the squad is self-organizing, they don't solely rely on the director or producer to assign tasks. The priorities are decided together then squad members are empowered to organize and manage their own work.

The person closest to the work has the autonomy to make choices based on their expertise. For example, if story changes are needed, execution of these can be deferred to the writer; if the pacing of the edit needs to be tightened, the editor can determine the best way forward.

This makes it possible to completely restructure how the work is done.

It doesn't have to be completed in a linear way but can be accomplished more efficiently by overlapping activities that go into making a film.

It also changes the power dynamics, giving everyone an equal voice and encouraging constructive conversations about ethics, inclusion, diversity and representation.

We've devised a range of practical activities, ceremonies and techniques that are integrated into the five-step method to foster teamwork and cooperation.

Fan focused first

We challenge the squad to see their film through the eyes of their fans, from inception to completion, for a compelling fan experience.

This is achieved by forging enduring connections with fans through ongoing research, interviews and practical tools so feedback can be timely and relevant.

The benefits of being fan focused include:
- × Not wasting time on elements that aren't important to fans
- × Assessing if a film is worth making
- × Improving the film before it's too expensive to make changes
- × Developing marketing and sales strategies while making the film
- × Retaining creative control over the final film

We use the term fan, rather than audience, which is too broad and generic for our purposes.

Fan
A person willing to invest their time, attention and money in a film. They're the ideal customer who will buy, watch and recommend the film. The squad gathers knowledge about these fans: their feelings, motivations and preferred means of communication.

The aim of the squad is to articulate the story they want to tell and find fans who want to see that story.

Knowing how many fans are interested in your film, and how to authentically communicate with them, ultimately determines the viability of the project.

It takes so much effort to make a film. After all the blood, sweat and tears, you want your film to be seen!

You can improve your chances of success by involving fans as early, and as often, as possible.

The squad validates their story ideas by conducting research first, then as the film goes through Make-Show-Adjust Cycles, fans give feedback on each version.

The goal is for the film to resonate so deeply with fans they'll ask, "How did you get inside my head like that?!"

Importantly, it's still the role of the squad to make creative decisions about the direction of the film. The squad listens and learns from fans, then they apply their skills and talent to execute any improvements.

The squad can make informed decisions about how to market and sell the film as they're the ones that have a relationship with the fans.

The squad is also best placed to make insightful changes based on early fan feedback to maintain the artistic value of the film.

Paradoxically, talking to fans allows the squad to retain more creative control.

Filmmakers normally only get feedback when the film is finished and "perfect". But by then it's too late. The film can't be improved with this feedback.

Even though showing people something raw and unfinished can feel terrifying, learning from fans in a timely way can transform the negative feelings associated with receiving feedback.

It inspires confidence to pursue a film with the knowledge it communicates as intended and is a worthwhile investment of time, energy and money.

Story before production values

We believe that powerful storytelling is intrinsic to the merit of films. Our creative effort is focused on validating the story first, then enhancing the film by adding production values.

This is achieved by testing assumptions via full-film drafts created through iterative Make-Show-Adjust Cycles and deferring investment in production values until the story has proven its appeal to fans.

There are many benefits of focusing on the story before production values, including:

- Not wasting time on unnecessary planning
- Making it easier to start, as a script isn't a prerequisite
- Reducing financial risk and costly waste, as budget is based on validated information
- Ensuring there's an audience for the film before any expensive investment

To *really* put the story before everything else, we've seriously re-evaluated the role of the script.

Conventional wisdom uses the script as a blueprint for what the final film could be and encourages decisions to be finalized in the development and pre-production stages of the filmmaking process.

Plot is decided.

Casting is decided.

Locations are decided.

Costumes, props, stunts and a thousand other things are all dictated by the script.

Scripts are littered with untested assumptions, forcing productions to budget for things that aren't needed and plan for circumstances that never eventuate.

It feels counterintuitive, but locking down ideas too early in a script makes us *less* creative.

We all get attached to ideas surprisingly quickly.

And once they're written down in a formal document, like a script, we're even more reluctant to make changes, take creative risks and discard weak ideas, even if it will improve the film.

A script is a technical document used as a proxy for the eventual film.

A script has a completely different format than a film, with different objectives. It's too easy to write a scene without worrying about how it will be executed or eventually perceived by fans.

The quality of the story comes into sharp relief when it can't be hidden behind well-crafted words on a page (or glossy production values). The faster a lo-fi film draft is made, the sooner the squad can start solving complex story challenges that are easily overlooked in the script format.

A mastery of writing and understanding of structure and character development are still essential skills and crucial to the success of the film. It's just that a script isn't the only way to use this expertise.

The writer works in the squad to validate the story and test assumptions by creating draft versions of the full film in Make-Show-Adjust Cycles, instead of polishing a script in isolation.

Making lo-fi film drafts encourages experimentation with little financial risk, while finding fans and letting them guide how high the production values need to be for an enjoyable film.

But the final film isn't inherently lo-fi or even low budget.

Production values are still important!

They just come later.

Initially the focus is discovering the essence of the story, developing a story using all of the creative disciplines and finding fans who want to experience that story. Expensive production values are incorporated once the story functions on all of these levels.

Learn by doing

We believe there's no substitute for hands-on learning experiences. The squad actively gains insights by doing the work, rather than wasting time on excessive documentation and arbitrary planning.

This is achieved by embedding continuous learning into the process, providing regular opportunities for the squad to adjust their ideas based on outcomes and shifting away from perfection towards experimentation.

The benefits of learning by doing include:
- Reducing onerous paperwork
- Increasing flexibility to make bold creative choices
- Sharing knowledge by working collaboratively in a squad
- Making decisions based on results rather than guesswork

Traditional filmmaking relies on piles of paperwork as a way to organize tasks.

There's the script, but also call sheets, shot lists, continuity forms and location agreements, just to name a few examples. The sheer amount of upfront planning can stifle creativity and create a high-stakes environment with little appetite for disruptions to the schedule.

In Lean Filmmaking, the focus is on doing the work, not wasteful planning.

The squad continuously learns by making more and more refined versions of the film through Make-Show-Adjust Cycles.

Working in ongoing iterative cycles provides the creative freedom to experiment before it's too hard or expensive to make meaningful changes.

In the earlier cycles, simplicity is favored over complex technology, gear or documentation that may impede flexibility.

This iterative process gives the squad time to reflect and consider how to improve their film and the way they work together, without the pressure of doing everything perfectly.

Make-Show-Adjust Cycles

Most traditional filmmaking methods follow a linear process that includes five stages: development, pre-production, production, post-production and distribution.

Work can't progress to the next stage until the previous one is completed.

The audience is only included in the final stage, if at all.

Lean Filmmaking is an iterative method that completes all of this work in Make-Show-Adjust (MSA) Cycles.

The work of planning, filming and learning is organized into small continuous cycles.

Squads use basic cycles to produce tester videos, then standard cycles for full-film drafts and polishes, before converging on the final version of the film.

The Make stage includes all the work required to complete a version of a tester video or the full film, the Show stage screens this to fans and the Adjust stage uses fan feedback and squad learnings to decide improvements for the next cycle.

MSA Cycles bring the core values to life.

All members of the squad are included in cycles so they can learn and improve together.

Cycles provide a framework for squads to work collaboratively within their constraints, using the skills, resources and experience of everyone in the squad.

Making versions of the full film provides a powerful way to understand what's working and what's not, in the medium of the intended output.

The structure of cycles make it easier to delay high production costs. Once the story works, production values can be targeted for the biggest impact.

Cycles help test the story with fans to determine the viability of a film, rather than wasting time on something that doesn't have any support.

The squad can make informed decisions based on results. They can creatively investigate all aspects of their film, focusing on experimentation over perfection.

Make
The squad makes a tester video or version of the full film, albeit lo-fi in the earlier cycles, including writing, directing, acting, shooting and editing. Some planning

is involved but only enough to make the work of the current cycle possible.

Show
A version of the tester video or full film is shown to fans for feedback through screenings, interviews, surveys and online data. In earlier cycles, conducting one-on-one interviews helps to understand the worldview of fans.

Adjust
The squad uses the learnings from making and showing the tester video or full film to collectively decide fan experience improvements for the next cycle. The squad identifies ways to optimize their team performance and continuously improve the workflow.

Repeat
The cycle starts again. The squad determines how many cycles are required depending on their shared goals. If the squad can't find fans, they pivot to a new story, test a different cohort of fans or abandon the film altogether.

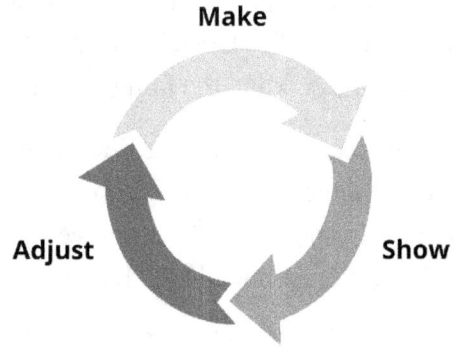

Imagine the terror when we announced at the Filmmakathon that we'd be doing four MSA Cycles in a weekend. It was such a departure from how the participants had ever made short films before.

They organized themselves into two squads of six people. Each squad had a production manager, writer/director, cinematographer, editor and two actors.

On Friday night they developed an idea for a short film from scratch. The output for the first cycle was a basic storyboard with a voice over, shot in one take with smartphones.

On Saturday, the second cycle was a lo-fi draft finished in three hours, and then a longer block of five hours to complete another draft for the third cycle.

On Sunday the squads had five hours to polish the final version in the fourth cycle, before screening their films to family, friends and fans.

Rather than spending too much time writing a script or planning a detailed shoot, the focus was on executing the most basic version of the idea in the simplest way, getting feedback and refining the film through cycles.

The squads used Lean Filmmaking techniques for transparent communication, creative problem-solving and informed decision-making. This allowed the squads to learn and improve, even while working within stringent constraints.

Values can transform creativity

We never thought that having core values could transform how we feel about creativity.

But it has.

These values are not prescriptive, inflexible rules, but rather a framework to see the creative process through a different lens.

Filmmakers basically spend all day, every day, making thousands of tiny decisions that eventually add up to a film.

We can't tell you how to make all of these decisions. Instead we've created the core values.

Let them be an anchor when you start losing yourself in the murky depths of decision-making fatigue.

We saw these core values transform how films can be made with our own eyes during the Filmmakathon.

The popcorn was served, the lights went down and the films flickered on the big screen.

We did a reverse screening of both squads' films – starting with the last cycle and working our way back to the first cycle. Even though the squads had to learn this new way of filmmaking, and had countless constraints, they still produced totally watchable films.

The cumulative effect of watching all of the versions back-to-back was a powerful demonstration of what can be achieved in a short time with the right process.

Our biggest takeaway from doing cycles for the first time was how quickly the squads adapted to the method once they felt the benefits for themselves, despite being skeptical that it would work.

The objective of the Filmmakathon was to validate the efficacy of the Lean Filmmaking method, rather than make award-winning films, but we were blown away by the results.

Experiencing the core values and MSA Cycles working together in a real-life experiment gave us the confidence to keep refining the method and eventually run an accelerator program to develop independent feature films.

What you need to start (and it isn't money)

Now you have a solid understanding of our philosophy, in the next part of this book we'll take you through the five-step Lean Filmmaking method for making independent feature films.

If you're ready to make your independent feature film a reality, you don't need:
- × A perfect script
- × A distribution deal
- × A shit-ton of money

Instead you'll need:
- × A squad of three to nine collaborators
- × Consistent chunks of time to do the work
- × The willingness to question everything you know about filmmaking

We encourage you to embrace the mystery of discovery, pursue experimentation, cultivate open-mindedness and foster playful creativity.

Best of all, you don't need to have all the answers before starting. Let's jump in!

Part 2: Step by Step Guide

The Lean Filmmaking Method

We've spoken to thousands of filmmakers with one thing in common: a burning desire to make their feature film.

But it seems like an impossible dream.

There are so many hurdles to jump over. Writing a script. Finding a producer. Getting funding. Securing distribution. Let alone having the financial means to support yourself for years while making this happen.

No wonder most independent filmmakers feel like this goal is out of reach.

We wanted to change that with the Lean Filmmaking method for creating independent feature films.

That's not to say it'll be easy.

In fact, sometimes it might *feel* harder because it's such a dramatic departure from how films are normally made.

We've purposely front-loaded the method with some of the toughest things to get right, like forming a well-balanced squad, finding passionate fans and validating the idea.

The initial steps don't cost much money, lowering the financial barriers for starting a project, but they still require a lot of effort.

Our goal is to offer an alternative pathway to creating films that increases the likelihood of success and is accessible to everyone.

We've spent years researching, investigating and testing this method. Along the way we've heard every single reason why it won't work.

We get it. A lot of these ideas seem counterintuitive.

If it's any consolation, some of our biggest detractors have become our strongest advocates once they put the method into practice for themselves and had positive results.

There are many benefits of the Lean Filmmaking method, including:
- × Increasing creativity
- × Empowering talent
- × Deepening fan engagement
- × Minimizing the risk of a flop
- × Reducing the fear of starting
- × Making more films, more often
- × Taking control of projects (and your career)

In this section, we show you how to make an independent feature film, from development to distribution, by following our five-step method.

Step 1: Form Squad
Working in a squad fundamentally changes filmmaking. The skills, talents and resources of the combined squad members determine the film that will be made, rather than a script or preconceived budget.

In this step, we talk about the benefits of a collaborative workflow, recruitment considerations, goal alignment and minimum viable squads.

Step 2: Discover Fans
A film needs a compelling reason to exist, an idea that deeply resonates with fans and the squad.

In this step, we discuss practical ways to identify early fans, conduct research interviews, make tester videos, get feedback and start validating the fan experience.

Step 3: Develop Drafts
It's crucial to find a connection between a story worth telling and the fans who want to see it.

In this step, we use Make-Show-Adjust Cycles to create full-film drafts that put the story front and center. We show you how to run these cycles efficiently, including how to overlap activities, write fan experience improvements, run squad ceremonies and find Story–Fan Fit.

Step 4: Produce Polishes
It's pivotal to find the connection between a well-crafted film and the fans who want to buy it.

In this step, we use Make-Show-Adjust Cycles to create full-film polishes to add production values that enhance the film's viability in the marketplace. We also discuss how to scale the squad, run paid feedback screenings and find Production–Fan Fit.

Step 5: Launch Film
To launch a film, it's important to communicate the fan experience through distribution channels and marketing campaigns that consistently sell the film.

In this step, we investigate self-distribution channels, discuss how to run marketing and sales experiments and go through the logistics of launching.

We encourage you to read the entire guide for an overview of the five steps before applying them to your own project.

As already mentioned, Lean Filmmaking is applicable to all types of film and video projects but this guide is specifically about creating an independent feature film.

To help illustrate the five steps, we'll use examples from a hypothetical narrative feature film, called *Solo Woman Traveler*, based on our experience coaching squads while testing the Lean Filmmaking method.

The Lean Filmmaking Method

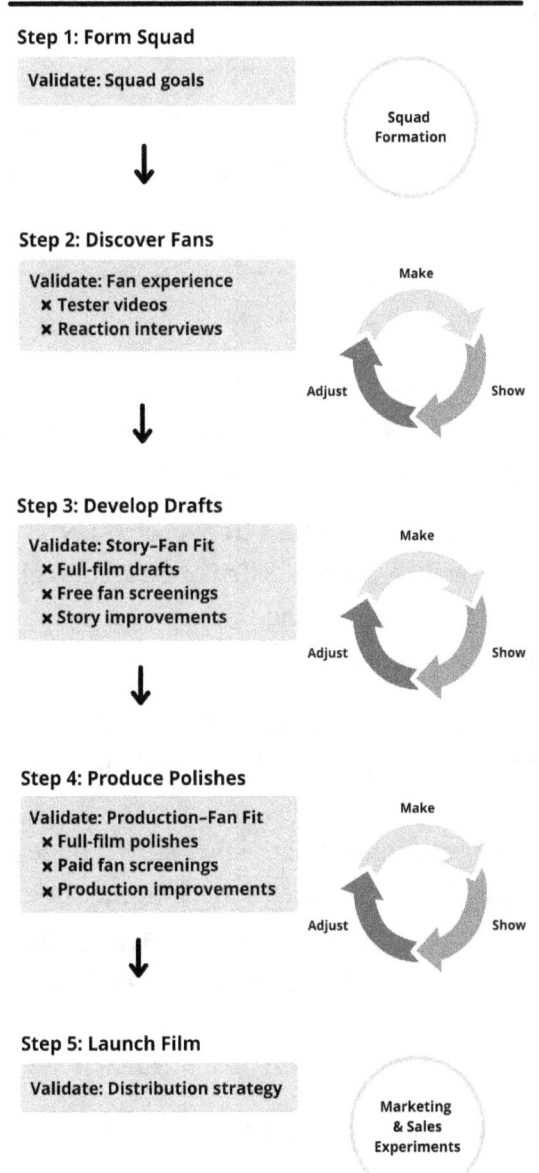

We'll also use anecdotes from our inaugural Independent Feature Film Accelerator for real-life examples of the Lean Filmmaking method in practice.

In the accelerator, two squads developed their debut micro-budget features in fifteen weeks, around day jobs.

Time Apart is a sci-fi romantic drama by producer Melanie Rowland and writer/director Ric Forster at Lilydale Films.

Trench is a film noir comedy thriller by producer/writer/actor Perri Cummings and producer/writer/director Paul Anthony Nelson at Cinema Viscera.

These two films are different from each other in almost every way, making them excellent case studies about how the Lean Filmmaking method works regardless of genre, style or artistic choices.

After participating in the accelerator, both squads subsequently completed, and launched, their films.

"The momentum needed to start such a huge project is daunting but if you have a method that takes you through the process, you'll find a way to actually do it." —Melanie Rowland, producer *Time Apart*

We believe that constraints breed creativity.

No fancy camera? Use your phone to start.

Don't have a big crew? A small squad can move fast to take advantage of opportunities.

No money? Solve problems with ingenuity instead of a cash firehose.

There's something liberating about embracing what you've got. So let's get stuck into it.

Step 1: Form Squad

A squad is the creative force that brings a film to life. The combined skills, talents and resources of the squad members ultimately determine the outcome of the film.

The first step in the Lean Filmmaking method is forming a well-aligned and motivated squad.

As well as the benefits gained from working collaboratively, there are other advantages to forming a squad first, including:
- Reducing bureaucracy for a streamlined workflow
- Building trust without the pressure of a do-or-die shoot
- Being prudent with resources to avoid over-producing
- Decreasing ineffectual upfront planning based on the script
- Developing a shared artistic vision and common goals

As defined in Part 1, squads are self-organizing, non-hierarchical and cross-functional teams of three to nine people that have the skills required to make a film.

The Lean Filmmaking Method

Step 1: Form Squad

Validate: Squad goals

↓

Step 2: Discover Fans

Validate: Fan experience
- Tester videos
- Reaction interviews

↓

Step 3: Develop Drafts

Validate: Story-Fan Fit
- Full-film drafts
- Free fan screenings
- Story improvements

↓

Step 4: Produce Polishes

Validate: Production-Fan Fit
- Full-film polishes
- Paid fan screenings
- Production improvements

↓

Step 5: Launch Film

Validate: Distribution strategy

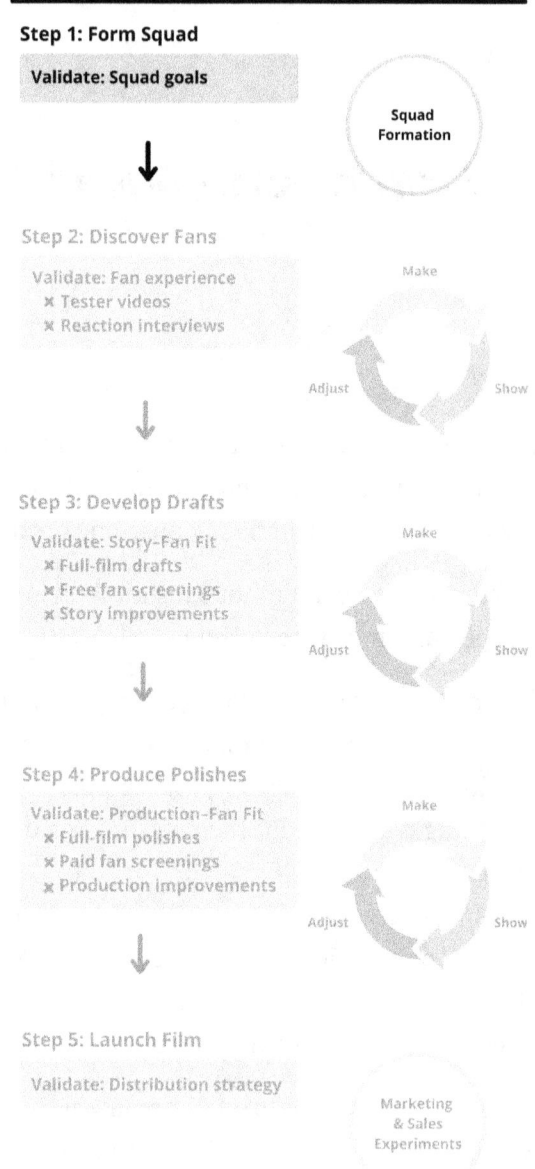

All members of the squad need experience in their specific area of expertise, but it's useful to have a wide breadth of knowledge about all aspects of filmmaking. You're looking for generalists, rather than specialists.

Every squad member will probably have diverse work experience outside of the film industry that could assist with the project, for example, marketing, financial planning, graphic design or legal knowledge. Along the way you may discover people's (often untapped) skills in unexpected areas that can be put to good use as well.

But a well-balanced squad isn't just about the right technical skills.

Characteristics like being curious, open-minded, solution-oriented and tenacious are just as important.

These traits help form a squad that has a sense of psychological safety.

A squad that feels psychologically safe takes risks, asks questions, seeks understanding and embraces creativity, without getting defensive, making excuses or being afraid of failure. All squad members can express themselves candidly in an environment of mutual respect, without fear of repercussions or negative consequences.

The success of the project takes priority over individual gains, so everyone needs to be a team player whose overarching desire is to make a film that provides value for the fans.

In the coming steps we'll outline specific activities, ceremonies and techniques that foster this high level of teamwork and cooperation. But in this step, let's focus on the significance of forming a squad before writing a script, recruiting considerations and the benefits of Go/No Go Meetings.

Start with a squad, not a script

It's been drilled into us that the first step in making a film is writing the perfect script – but actually, this belief can be the biggest barrier to getting started.

It's easy to spend years writing, rewriting and polishing a script yet still be no closer to production. There's a reason why Hollywood calls it development hell.

A more insidious side effect of writing the script first is that it stifles creativity and collaboration.

A script locks in requirements, like ambitious locations, difficult stunts or very specific casting, making it practically impossible to start pre-production without a large upfront financial investment. Projects are indefinitely stalled until these complex moving parts magically fall into place.

By the time the cast and crew are finally on board, the big-ticket items have been decided and true collaboration is limited. There's little flexibility to explore, experiment or trash crappy ideas.

Nevermind the additional downside of writing elements into scripts that haven't been validated with fans, wasting precious time, money and energy.

If you want to use the Lean Filmmaking method to produce an already existing script, we've got some bad news.

The longer the script has been in development, the more challenging this method will feel.

That's not to say it can't be done.

Just be prepared to throw away your hard work if the squad discovers new ideas that serve the film better.

Please don't misunderstand this. Scripts can still be useful. They just happen at a different time and potentially in a different format.

Also, scripts aren't the only way to express a story for the screen. And they certainly don't have to be the only starting point.

It's much easier to come up with film ideas than it is to find creative collaborators. Form the squad first, then they can tackle the story together.

Recruit for skills, not roles

To keep the squad small, people will ideally have several skills and be a multi-passionate creative, for example, writer/producer/marketer, writer/director/actor or cinematographer/editor/producer.

Squad members can also contribute in ways that aren't limited to official job titles.

The essential core skills for a squad include:
- Producing
- Writing
- Directing
- Acting
- Shooting
- Editing
- Marketing
- Coaching

Obviously there are many other skills normally required to produce a film, like set design, hair and makeup, prop-making, stunt coordination, location management, continuity, music composition, color grading – the list goes on...and on...and on.

But Lean Filmmaking starts with the most basic lo-fi version of the film, gradually adding elements in MSA Cycles, after validating with fans to verify that they're important.

In the early MSA Cycles, everyone has to chip in.

The actors might do their own makeup, the cinematographer also does sound recording, the director can organize locations. This allows the work of making a film to remain fast-paced, fluid and agile.

For example, one of the squads in the accelerator made their feature film *Time Apart* with only three people (excluding supporting actors). As experienced filmmakers, they had the skills, talent and tenacity required to make the film with such a small squad.

"I produced the film. But under that umbrella also fell locations, costume, continuity, scheduling, sound recording..." —Melanie Rowland, producer *Time Apart*

"I wrote, directed, shot, lit and edited it – if you'd asked me if I wanted to be the director of photography on my own feature, I'd have said no way. But it was one of the good things that came out during this process. [...] We realized we could do it with a tiny number of people." —Ric Forster, writer/director *Time Apart*

In a squad, everyone is on board for the whole process.

They work together end-to-end, through development, pre-production, production, post-production and distribution. All of this work is done in MSA Cycles, rather than in a linear process.

Just because the squad is cross-functional, doesn't mean that roles don't exist.

It's up to the squad how to decide whose skills are best suited for what role and how the work is allocated, allowing for a high degree of flexibility. The roles can also be adapted over time as the squad learns more about their workflow through MSA Cycles.

For example, if the squad member who normally directs is required to help finish an edit, the person who normally writes can direct some scenes. The editor might need to fill in as a background actor in a scene, an actor might need to write dialogue for a scene and everyone needs to interview fans.

This workflow provides transparency into everyone's creative process and a favorable environment for people to do their best work. It sparks curiosity about other areas of expertise, gives a deeper understanding of colleagues' challenges and creates opportunities to learn about every part of filmmaking.

Choose the minimum viable squad (it's smaller than you think)

It's crucial to find the minimum number of people to form a well-balanced squad.

We recommend that the squad is between three to nine people. (More than five can still be pretty unwieldy if you're trying Lean Filmmaking for the first time, so this is probably the top end for newbies.)

The smaller the squad, the easier it is to communicate clearly, work fast and stay agile.

Even with ambitious plans, you only need a few squad members in the beginning.

A benefit of working in MSA Cycles is that aspirational goals aren't an impediment to starting. The squad can gradually build up to these goals as they learn more about their fans, and the story they are trying to tell.

In traditional filmmaking, often the first solution to any problem is to throw more money at it.

We need more hands on deck; hire more runners! Get a script doctor; they'll figure this shit out! We're going to miss a deadline; bring in *everyone* and work around the clock to get it done!

The negative impact of hiring more people is nearly always downplayed and what can be achieved is exaggerated.

The complexities of scale created by working in large teams are managed by hiring department heads, formalizing hierarchical structures and mandating comprehensive documentation.

This inefficiency creates demand for more people, which creates more inefficiency.

Every additional person exponentially increases the chances that the wrong work will get done. Much of the paperwork produced on film sets is about making sure everyone is in the same place, at the same time, doing the right thing that's required at that moment.

But when there's only a few people to organize, there's no need for elaborate schedules, call sheets or shot lists.

This instantly reduces tedious administration duties and cuts down time spent on paperwork.

Obviously health and safety procedures, permits and insurance policies are still important. People's well-being is more important than any film. Some paperwork is impossible to avoid for good reason. But even these essential requirements are easier to manage with a small squad.

We recommend only increasing the size of the squad as an act of last resort: when an obvious pain exists and overcoming the additional challenges are justified.

This doesn't rule out hiring more cast for supporting roles or crew for specialist tasks as the film progresses. (Scaling beyond the squad is discussed in Step 4).

When the work is fundamentally creative, and the squad has already bonded, adding squad members may not be the ideal solution. Embrace the inherent constraints of a small squad and let go of the illusion that a bigger team will solve every problem.

In our hypothetical example, *Solo Woman Traveler*, we were a squad of four with two actors, a director/shooter/editor and a producer/marketer/coach. Everyone had writing experience, and the actors were skilled in improvisation, so this work was a collaborative effort. At some point everyone lugged gear, held a mic or camera and found fans to interview.

The small size of this squad made it simple to coordinate meeting times, manage workload and ensure everyone's full participation in the creative output.

In the first instance, as we all had day jobs, we met at the same central location two nights a week from 5pm to 8pm for three months. (As you'll see in the next steps, we made good progress on the film just with weekly meetings and the occasional weekend.)

Most tasks were completed during our meetings but sometimes administration jobs, like coordinating fan interviews or research, had to be done as homework. These jobs were kept to a minimum and we often asked ourselves if we were being too ambitious, if there was a simpler way or if it needed to be done at all.

We'd spend a few minutes at the beginning and end of each meeting to plan our work.

This made communication super easy. We already knew our schedule! All conversations and activity coordination happened in an online group chat.

The two squads in the Independent Feature Film Accelerator were even smaller. Both squads only had three members: two crew and one key actor.

We had an ambitious goal to develop three full-film drafts during the fifteen weeks of the program, so this was a much more intense schedule.

We kicked off with a Filmmakathon weekend for both squads to practice Lean Filmmaking fundamentals, then held weekly two-hour masterclasses to teach the method in more detail. Over the duration of the accelerator, we coached the squads through MSA Cycles and provided feedback, support and accountability.

"The weekly masterclasses on developing, refining, making and remaking the film were challenging, but endlessly invigorating and motivating." —Perri Cummings and Paul Anthony Nelson, producers *Trench*

Outside of the masterclasses, the squads managed their own time to complete the weekly tasks and had rigorous schedules, working on their films most nights and weekends. We'd only recommend this strategy for short bursts as it's unsustainable in the longer term.

Align squad goals

Before the newly formed squad embarks on this journey together, it's important to make sure there's a shared goal.

Often the underlying goal of an independent film is screening at a prestigious festival where fame and fortune await.

Sure, festivals have their benefits but being accepted isn't in the squad's control, especially for a debut feature without a distributor. (We've got a lot more to say about festivals as a distribution strategy in Step 5.)

In Lean Filmmaking, the goals can be simple but they need to be tangible.

For a project to be successful, the goals should target the intersection of what the squad creatively wants to achieve, what constraints they are working within and what fans want to see.

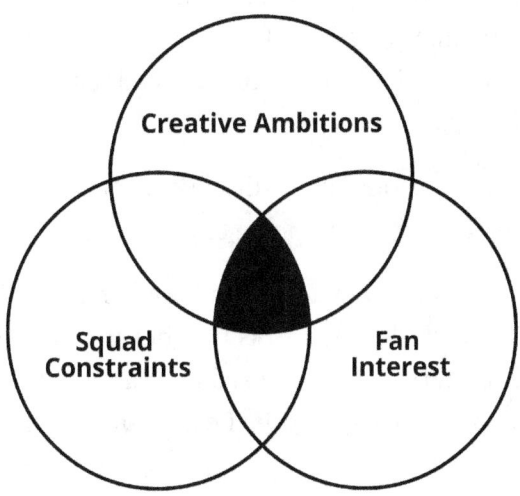

It's important for the squad to be passionate about their creative ambition for the project. It should be a shared interest that all squad members are willing to explore, like a genre, style, subject matter, theme or even an aspirational vision.

The project is unlikely to get very far without interest from fans. The film must connect with fans who have demonstrated a strong desire to buy it, watch it and recommend it to others. The more niche, the better.

It's crucial to consider the squad's specific constraints, like whether they already own any gear, the amount of time available to work on the film and any existing cash reserves. But it could also include other resources like special talents (actors who can dance, speak a second language or sword fight), additional skills (writer who is also a graphic designer) or free access to elements that add production value (unique locations or unusual props).

If you're stuck about how to discover shared goals, we suggest using Affinity Mapping to get started.

Affinity Mapping is a practical and powerful tool that quickly generates ideas, sparks insights and uncovers thematic patterns. It can be used in a variety of circumstances throughout the Lean Filmmaking method and it's simple to do.

In this case, the squad can use the Project Success Target as a place to start.

Set a timer for three minutes. Everyone silently writes sticky notes, using each circle of the diagram to spark ideas.

Each person then takes turns putting their sticky notes up on a wall or whiteboard, briefly describing each one without interruption from the other squad members. Any similar ideas can be grouped together.

When all the sticky notes are up, the squad discusses, rearranges and sorts the ideas into clusters that have an affinity with each other. As patterns appear, the groupings can be categorized and labeled.

The squad expands on the groupings by repeating the process.

The squad can do multiple rounds, diving deeper until enough ideas have been generated to formulate the squad goals.

For example, the *Solo Woman Traveler* squad spent an hour Affinity Mapping. We discovered a shared interest in free-spirited solo world travel and the collective desire to tell a story with a strong woman protagonist. We decided that our goal was to showcase a positive representation of a solo woman traveler (and this became a placeholder for the film's title).

Once the squad has a general agreement about their goals, it's helpful to broadly discuss the financial responsibilities for the project and ownership of the film.

In the traditional filmmaking process, the budget for the film is decided based on the script and amount of funding that can be raised.

But in Lean Filmmaking we postpone spending money until the story is validated with fans.

At this point, it's more important that all squad members agree about their time commitment, often referred to as sweat equity, rather than any substantial cash investment.

Sweat equity is a fancy way of saying everyone contributes their free labor, as opposed to financial equity, which is a contribution of capital. The gratis work of the squad directly increases the value of the film for their mutual benefit.

"When making their first project, a lot of producers fall into a funding trap, [...] stuck in a loop of trying to get money. But you can do it without funding. Get a small squad and just start." —Melanie Rowland, producer *Time Apart*

It's beneficial to acknowledge the squad's interest in making the film may be non-financial.

Maybe they're trying to spread awareness about a social message, expand their credibility as artists, or reach a wide audience to build a relationship for future projects.

It's up to the squad to determine what success looks like for them.

Every squad will have different considerations but some things to discuss include:

- Whether squad members will share equally in the risks and rewards
- Whether squad members will work for sweat equity, deferred payment or profit share
- How the intellectual property and copyright of the film will be managed
- How expenses and income will be managed
- How effort will be recognized if squad members leave before the film is completed

Don't use these questions as a justification to slow the squad's progress. Try to keep it simple.

Perhaps all of the squad members just sign basic release forms. Maybe they set up a company, become a cooperative or seek independent legal advice.

There are no perfect answers, or one right way of doing this!

Our squad spent several hours discussing the basic parameters of *Solo Woman Traveler*. We decided to have an equal partnership with all squad members sharing the risks and rewards, committed to weekly meetings for at least three months with no pay (sweat equity) and any expense over $50 would be approved by everyone before purchasing.

Aligning the squad's goals is about practicing having candid conversations, building trust and managing expectations.

As the squad works through the next steps, their goals can be refined or adapted as new information becomes available.

A squad needs transparency and moxie

Starting with a squad radically changes the entire filmmaking process.

This is a *very* transparent way of working.

It's scary at first. It can feel like a loss of control.

But the cross-functional structure of the squad, the four core values and framework of MSA Cycles make this level of transparency possible.

It also helps to have a good dose of moxie! It takes courage, nerve and determination to re-examine every element of filmmaking.

To maximize collaboration, two big paradigm shifts are required for squad members:
- × The director doesn't have authority to give unilateral commands
- × The cast and crew have autonomy and take responsibility for their area of expertise

Everyone contributes to the project by making informed decisions and understanding the implications for the entire film. MSA Cycles allow the squad to learn what's working and experiment with what can be improved.

In traditional filmmaking, all of the departments are in silos and compete for a larger piece of the budget, often to the detriment of the final film. Department heads are forced to competitively pitch to the director, or producer, for resources they believe will make the film successful, without any context into the overall impact of their recommendations.

And because the film industry currently hires cast and crew based on credits, and a showreel of previous work, this can skew priorities during the production. It's possible to win a prestigious award for a specific craft, like cinematography, costume design or special effects, in a film that by all other measures is a failure.

This is not the fault of hardworking cast and crew who are genuinely doing their best within a flawed system.

It's an unfortunate by-product of the traditional filmmaking process that pits specialties against each other and emphasizes individual performance over true collaboration.

Lean Filmmaking changes this by breaking down silos and the hierarchical structure, to help the squad recognize what's best for the project as a whole. It also allows the fans' perspective to be given serious consideration.

Rather than making decisions based on things like "A cool drone shot will look awesome in my showreel", it becomes "Does this drone shot take priority over other improvements as determined by the squad?" and "Does this drone shot improve the fan experience?"

This doesn't mean that squad consensus is always required.

It's unrealistic for everyone to agree at all times.

Different skills can take the lead at different times.

When there's dissent, defer to the squad member who is closest to the work with the most experience in the first instance. For example, if it's about the pacing of a visual montage then the person with the editing skills makes the decision, or if it's going to impact a character's backstory then the person who is acting decides.

If there's a difference of opinion, choose one of the ideas to execute in the next MSA Cycle – then if it doesn't work, another idea can be explored in the following cycle.

Traditional film productions can be toxic environments with rampant pressure to perform challenging work in tough conditions. Long hours, demanding schedules and unrealistic deadlines are the norm.

But Lean Filmmaking is non-linear, opening up new opportunities to make meaningful work in sustainable, responsible and thoughtful ways.

It's also non-hierarchical and provides a framework to question practices, values and ethics, rather than normalizing unacceptable behaviors. This structure gives squad members permission to speak up and make filmmaking safer for everyone.

Special notes for directors

The most common objection to the flat structure of squads is that the creative vision is no longer only in the hands of the director.

A creative vision is crucial for a successful film, but all squad members have input.

The director can still passionately explore a theme or concept, but they can't be locked into a singular way of executing their idea. Rather, by drawing on the expertise of the squad and gaining insight from fans, they can embrace different ways to bring the film to life.

We've found this to be artistically liberating.

Normally the director spends months (or years) accounting for every possible scenario, leaving nothing to chance and making pivotal creative choices, before even getting on set.

But with Lean Filmmaking, the director doesn't need to have all the answers or plan out everything perfectly. Instead they can learn as they go, ask thoughtful questions, keep an open mind and listen intently to the squad – and the fans – to creatively shape the film.

The director's role becomes more like that of a "servant leader", rather than a command and control, top-down micromanager.

The squad isn't formed to meet the demands of the director, instead the director serves the collective wishes of the squad.

The director is a loyal advocate for the squad and the film, providing a crucial big-picture perspective. They share their power, build trust and teamwork, put the needs of the story over their ego and embrace feedback from fans.

Special notes for writers

We know it seems disrespectful to encourage films to be made without a script. Especially as writers traditionally measure their contribution to the filmmaking process by delivering a script.

But the script isn't the final product of a film.

It's a blueprint: a technical document that's used as a proxy for the eventual film. Writing a script is not the same as writing a novel, poem or even song lyrics, that are all directly consumed by an audience.

Writers' contributions are often overlooked as film is considered a director's medium. Once they've completed the final draft, and the film goes into production, writers are unlikely to be included again. They're lucky to get an invite to the premiere screening!

In Lean Filmmaking, the writer is an integral part of the entire process. All of the craft skills, like character development, structure, plotting and dramatic tension, that go into writing a script are still essential – they're just applied in a different way.

The writer is the story ambassador. They guide the squad through the film's narrative structure and maintain the Story Scaffold. (The instructions for how to do this are in Step 3.)

There's another benefit for the writer. By seeing first-hand the direction, performances, camerawork and editing, the writer can experiment in an agile way. They don't need to spend months (or years) polishing words on a page in isolation without a real-world way to test what works best on screen.

Special notes for actors

Lean Filmmaking fundamentally changes the process for actors, especially casting.

An exhaustive search to find actors that fit predetermined roles as described in a script is no longer required.

Instead, the lead actors are "cast" when the squad is formed, then the film is specifically designed to take advantage of their skills, talents and expertise.

The actors have autonomy over their characters' backstories, motivations and actions, helping construct the story from the ground up. They're part of the process of making the whole film, working collaboratively alongside the other squad members, from beginning to end.

This method can be truly transformative for actors.

Actors get a deeper understanding of the technical considerations that impact their performance. For example, they see first-hand how the editor makes decisions about which takes are used and which are cut. These insights can quickly improve their acting skills.

Actors also receive feedback directly from fans, rather than filtered through another source like the director, allowing them to make informed creative choices about how to play their character in future MSA Cycles.

As actors participate equally in the decision-making process, they're not coerced to take unnecessary physical risks, endanger their mental health or participate in exploitative scenes. Ceremonies are in place for the squad to discuss issues, including those around on-screen intimacy and personal boundaries.

Special notes for cinematographers and editors

The biggest challenge for roles that are highly technical, like cinematographers and editors, is the speed of delivery and quick turnaround times. A fast and efficient workflow is crucial.

Working in MSA Cycles requires rigorous accountability, flexible agility and an understanding of the squad's constraints.

In the early cycles, it's more important to experiment than to get a beautiful shot or a seamless edit. There's no value in spending hours setting up elaborate lighting for a scene that will probably be trashed in the next cycle.

In an artform that demands perfection, this is a major change. We're not suggesting that quality isn't important. In fact, we believe that this method provides a higher level of quality with less waste, as the value is determined by fans.

It can be unnerving to have rough drafts judged by other squad members and to receive feedback directly from fans, but the benefits far outweigh the initial discomfort.

Lean Filmmaking allows creative exploration of the technical elements that can deeply enhance the narrative. If the story connects with fans in rough draft versions, by the time production values are carefully added, the film is taken to an even higher level.

Special notes for the Lean Filmmaking coach

Hate to break it to you but if you're reading this book, it's most likely you'll be the Lean Filmmaking coach for your squad.

In the beginning, as the squad learns the Lean Filmmaking method, the coach teaches the core values and provides guidance through the five steps.

The coach is also responsible for advising on MSA Cycles and running ceremonies, like standups, reviews and retrospectives. (The instructions for how to do this are in Step 3.)

It takes a couple of MSA Cycles to really get into the flow. Once everyone feels more confident with the method, coaching is still required to ensure continuous improvement is being made – both with the film and the way the squad works together.

Being a coach is one of the many hats you'll wear while making the film. It's a rewarding but demanding undertaking. Coaching requires patience, perseverance and ability to keep moving forward in the face of ambiguity.

A common challenge that coaches have when using the Lean Filmmaking method for the first time is that the squad can't fully appreciate the advantages without having experienced it for themselves.

It feels easier to skip steps because they sound like a waste of time, and sometimes even seem counterproductive. The pressure to start production straight away will be *strong*.

There's a tendency to fall back on old habits when the going gets tough.

And it'll get tough! (Where's that moxie when you need it?)

The coach is a torchbearer who provides crucial support to the squad, reassuring them that growing pains are part of the process and that it gets easier with practice.

Go/No Go Meetings help when forming a squad (and while making the film)

It's a big commitment to make a feature film, especially when using an unfamiliar method like Lean Filmmaking with new people.

So give everyone an easy escape hatch.

One way to do this is with Go/No Go Meetings.

A Go/No Go Meeting is held at a predetermined time when the squad decides whether or not to continue work on the film by frankly assessing the pros and cons.

Set a timer for three minutes. Everyone silently writes sticky notes about their personal reasons for going ahead or not.

Each person then takes a turn to put their sticky notes up on a wall or whiteboard under the heading of pro or con, briefly describing each one to the squad. This is not the time for debate; let everyone voice their ideas without interruption.

When all the sticky notes are up, the whole squad can discuss and decide the best way forward.

This meeting is an opportunity for every squad member to honestly share their reasons for proceeding, or stopping, while evaluating if it's still worth investing time, energy and resources into the project.

And it's got to be okay to call it quits!

There may be legitimate reasons for not proceeding with the film anymore. Or for individual members of the squad to leave the project.

It can be useful for the first Go/No Go Meeting to be shortly after forming the squad, like six weeks, before everyone commits to a longer timeframe.

Running this meeting at the end of each step is also an excellent stop-gap to help make realistic decisions about everyone's emotional capacity, time constraints and financial commitment.

You're done with this step when...

You have a squad.

It's well balanced, with compatible values and a great mix of expertise.

You've started building trust with open communication, aligned goals and a shared understanding about the ownership of the film.

Finally, you need to determine how the next step will be resourced.

It's likely that everyone will still be unpaid. Time, not cash, is the most important resource for the next step. Given this, the squad needs to determine a regular meeting schedule so the work can be done.

Some basic tester videos will be made in the next step but we *strongly* encourage you to spend the least amount of money possible, preferably zero dollars.

If you're even thinking about splashing cash, you're adding production values too early. Instead, work within your constraints, use gear you already own and take advantage of free tools.

Lean into your creativity!

If you can complete the checklist below, and understand the tools, you're ready to move on.

Step 1 Checklist
- × Recruit squad members
- × Set squad goals
- × Confirm film ownership and financials
- × Set date for next Go/No Go Meeting
- × Commit to work schedule for the next step

Step 1 Tools
- × Go/No Go Meeting
- × Project Success Target
- × Affinity Mapping

Step 2: Discover Fans

A film needs a compelling reason to exist, an idea that resonates with fans and the squad.

The second step in the Lean Filmmaking method is to discover fans with research interviews and tester videos.

As well as the many advantages of being fan focused first, there are other benefits to discovering fans before going into production, including:
- × Practicing creative decision-making based on fan feedback
- × Learning to listen to criticism without defensiveness
- × Purposely experimenting with daring and outrageous ideas before investing resources

In traditional filmmaking, the typical rationale for making a film is to tell a specific story. Generally, a script is written based on an original story and produced without deviation from that idea.

The Lean Filmmaking Method

Step 1: Form Squad

Validate: Squad goals

Step 2: Discover Fans

Validate: Fan experience
- ✘ Tester videos
- ✘ Reaction interviews

Step 3: Develop Drafts

Validate: Story–Fan Fit
- ✘ Full-film drafts
- ✘ Free fan screenings
- ✘ Story improvements

Step 4: Produce Polishes

Validate: Production–Fan Fit
- ✘ Full-film polishes
- ✘ Paid fan screenings
- ✘ Production improvements

Step 5: Launch Film

Validate: Distribution strategy

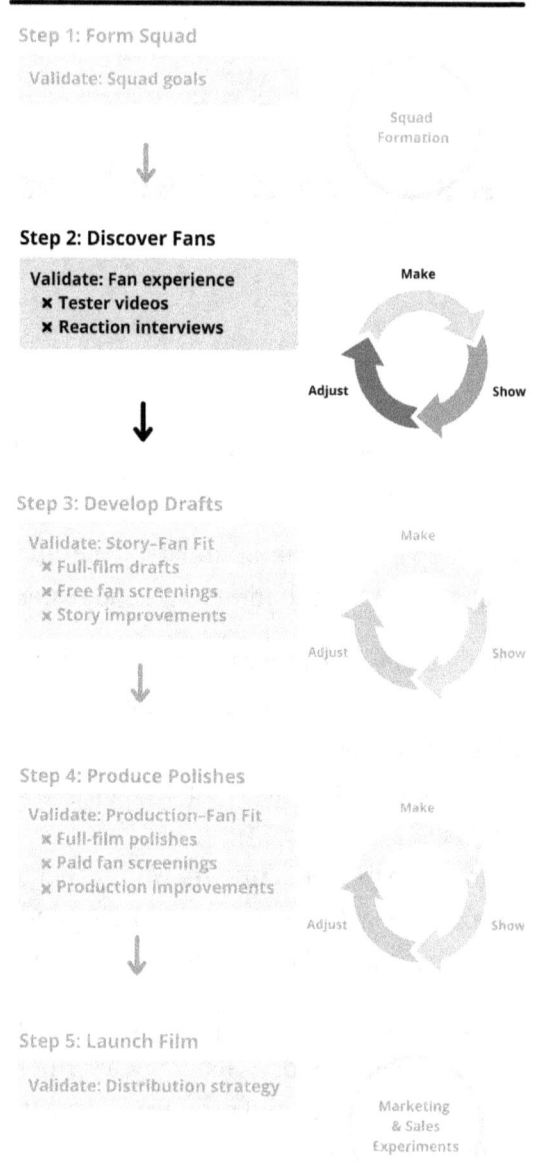

In Lean Filmmaking we're willing to revamp, pivot or discard ideas until we find the best interpretation of a story that connects with our fans. We validate our ideas with fans before investing time, money and energy in production.

We're focused on empowering independent filmmakers and encouraging more diverse stories to be told.

Appealing to a broad audience often relies on A-list star power and flashy production values, dramatically increasing the costs. This kind of high-stakes filmmaking is out of reach for the majority of people and disproportionately favors those with privilege and access.

As an indie filmmaker, you don't have the luxury of trying to reach everyone. Your film needs to be made just for your fans.

If your film successfully breaks out into different groups of people than expected, that's great. But fans are the first priority.

A fan can be identified by psychographics like values, interests and lifestyle (and not just simplistic demographics like age, income or gender).

A fan actively engages with a subculture or niche group (and isn't just part of a generic mainstream audience).

A fan emotionally cares about the subject of the film (and isn't just an industry peer or fellow filmmaker).

A fan is a person willing to invest their time, attention and money – the ideal customer who'll buy, watch and recommend this particular film.

The squad gathers knowledge about these fans: their feelings, motivations and preferred means of communication.

The goal is to find repeatable ways of recruiting fans and consistently converting them into taking action, whether it's giving feedback, sharing content or purchasing the film.

In Lean Filmmaking, it's our responsibility as filmmakers to find the fans for our own film.

It's not up to distributors, festivals and exhibitors.

It's up to us.

And that's exhilarating!

After all, if the squad makes insightful improvements based on early fan feedback, it allows them to retain creative control.

The squad can make informed decisions about marketing and selling the film as they have the relationship with fans.

This flies in the face of conventional filmmaking wisdom.

Filmmakers are routinely told that "pandering to an audience" will irreparably damage their artistic integrity.

That's blatantly not true.

It's just that most filmmakers get audience feedback at the wrong time – once their film is complete.

It's heartbreaking to hear negative feedback (even if it's constructive) at the end of the filmmaking process, because in all likelihood, the film can't be changed at this late stage.

Fan feedback needs to be received at the right time to make it worthwhile and preserve the artistic value of the film.

In Lean Filmmaking, fan feedback is enthusiastically acquired early and often. Collecting feedback is integrated into MSA Cycles, ensuring it's timely, useful and purposeful. The squad listens and learns from fans at the appropriate times, then they apply their skills, creativity and talent to improve the film.

This research helps the squad form educated estimates about the number of fans interested in the film, authentic ways to communicate with them and the viability of the project.

You don't have to reach *all* of your fans in the beginning. The squad just needs a small sample of fans to validate the idea, then they can gradually grow the fanbase during MSA Cycles.

Unfortunately, there's no simple one-size-fits-all way to find fans.

If this was an easy task, every film would find an audience with little effort.

The Lean Filmmaking method does this hard work upfront because we accept that finding fans is fundamental to releasing a successful independent film.

In this step we'll look at practical ways to identify early fans, conduct research interviews, define the fan experience and refine ideas with tester videos.

But before we go any further, let's address the elephant in the room...

Let's talk about talking to fans

Do your palms start sweating when you think about sharing your less-than-perfect idea?

Is your heart nervously beating faster at the very thought of asking for feedback?

Are you already coming up with great excuses in your head for skipping this step?

Don't worry, that's pretty normal.

After talking to thousands of filmmakers about the benefits of validating ideas, we're never surprised by the intense reaction to this step. It's understandable. There are justifiable fears around getting fan feedback.

Let's take a moment to deconstruct some common

objections filmmakers have about talking to fans.

I already know who my audience is...it's me

Filmmakers often think they're making their film for themselves, and like-minded people just like them, so they already know everything there is to know.

But this is a huge gamble.

If you're working for years and spending thousands of dollars to make a personal film, surely it'd be good to know if people want to see it? Fan research can help.

It's better to test the assumptions you've made about potential fans before wasting time, money and energy on a film no one wants to watch.

Even if you're an expert in the film's subject matter, you'll be surprised how much you can still learn from fans.

At the very least, you'll confirm your idea connects with fans, letting you proceed with confidence. It's reassuring to know there is more than an audience of one for your film.

I don't want to hear negative feedback

Here's the cold hard truth: audiences will have an opinion about your film, regardless of whether you talk to them or not.

If you only let people see the finished product, you've missed any opportunity to learn from them and make the film better.

Lean Filmmaking provides a formalized structure to solicit and interpret feedback, ensuring the information collected is timely, useful and purposeful.

"It changed our ability to listen to feedback. Early on you defend everything you've done, but if you can get past that and dissect what people are saying, you're able to improve the film." —Melanie Rowland, producer *Time Apart*

The more often you talk to fans, the easier it becomes. You'll get proficient at receiving even the harshest criticism – taking what you need from it and discarding the rest – without having to defend your creative choices.

I've got high standards

Filmmakers comfort themselves in the knowledge that producing an aesthetically beautiful and technically proficient film is still considered a success by their peers, even if it loses money and is barely seen outside a handful of festivals.

Even worse, a deeply held attachment to high standards can stop filmmakers from pursuing their dream, fearful that their film will never be good enough.

Sometimes high standards are just a really sneaky disguise for perfectionism.

In Lean Filmmaking, we adopt the motto "Done is better than perfect". Making a film in MSA Cycles allows us to learn by doing, rather than being endlessly trapped tweaking, polishing and obsessing without any input from the intended viewers.

We get feedback from fans to help us decide what's important to them (and what they couldn't care less about) and make decisions accordingly.

"Every time you show the film to people, they'll tell you what's important. You soon find out that things you think are really important aren't a big deal to your fans." —Paul Anthony Nelson, producer *Trench*

We respect high standards but believe the level of quality required for the film is determined by fans, rather than an arbitrary measure set by the industry.

I won't get any useful feedback without adding production values

As creatives, much of our work is judged on having impressive production values. It's how we build a showreel, get hired for gigs and measure our contribution to the artform.

It's easy to understand why we'd be nervous to share our ideas in their most raw state.

Why take the risk if we think fans won't "get it" unless they see the final bells-and-whistles execution of our idea?

But everyone these days is film-literate.

We have video cameras and sophisticated editing apps readily available on our phones and access to worldwide distribution through social media.

Besides, you're only after a small sample of fans – not everyone. Even with a very lo-fi version of the idea, you can get a ton of useful feedback.

Don't spend too long perfecting an idea; instead, quickly test it with a few fans to see if it sparks any interest in its roughest form.

Understanding the purpose of early feedback, and being able to receive criticism without defensiveness, can transform your creative practice.

I'll have to dumb it down for people to understand

Often it's studios, distributors and producers, not the fans, who want to "dumb it down" and make films more mainstream. After all, they're the ones with millions of dollars at risk and need to recoup their investment by appealing to a broad audience.

Most fans are smart, film-savvy consumers who can help make your film better than you ever imagined.

"Getting feedback meant having faith in the fans."
—Ric Forster, writer/director *Time Apart*

If anything, getting early feedback can make your film *less* mainstream.

Our first ideas can be unoriginal. This method allows us to move beyond clichés, delve into the nuance of our chosen theme and ensure the film communicates its intended meaning.

You're free to take creative risks, explore outrageous tangents and investigate interesting synchronicities, without high expectations or large amounts of money on the line.

I don't want to do test screenings

Hollywood test screenings normally happen at the end of the filmmaking process and their function is to determine a marketing strategy, not necessarily to improve the film.

Making meaningful changes is prohibitively expensive for most films at this late stage.

Instead, the feedback from these test screenings informs superficial refinements and shapes promotional materials, like the poster and trailer, used to market the film.

If any major changes are required, like shooting a new ending that appeals to a broader audience, the filmmaker may be forced to make them with threats of dumping the film onto the market without marketing support, or being indefinitely shelved, if not carried out.

Test screenings can become a battleground for creative control.

Lean Filmmaking doesn't advocate for these kinds of test screenings.

Rather, fan feedback is done continuously through MSA Cycles, making it timely, relevant and actionable. Marketing strategies are explored from the start of the project so won't be a rude surprise to anyone when it comes time to sell the film.

If I build it, they will come

This may have been the case in the past when gatekeepers limited the number of films produced and released each year, but now there's a firehose of content spraying in every direction.

As the tools of filmmaking – and the means of distribution – are democratized, there's increasing competition for people's attention.

If you go full steam ahead, with hopes and dreams that your film will magically find an audience once it's done, you're setting yourself up for a massive disappointment.

In Lean Filmmaking, instead of thinking about how fans will find the film at the very end of the process, we start testing marketing and sales strategies early to give squads the greatest chance of success.

"It was great discovering our fans early in the process and making the film a satisfying experience for them." —Perri Cummings, producer *Trench*

Research interviews give squads lots of juicy information about their fans that is instrumental when distributing the film. It determines the size of the fan group, giving a solid indication of how much to invest in the film and where to recoup this investment.

I'll be sacrificing my artistic vision

We've come full circle. We touched on it earlier but this fear comes up again and again.

Directors are lauded for their unwavering artistic vision. They rarely solicit audience critiques in a misguided attempt to maintain creative control. If anything, the only respected feedback comes from peers, or film industry insiders, not potential fans.

In Lean Filmmaking it's still vitally important to have an artistic vision, but it's shared by the whole squad, not just the director.

As the squad shows fans different versions of the film

at specific intervals in MSA Cycles, they interpret the feedback and creatively use it to strengthen the artistic vision and improve the overall quality of the film.

Paradoxically, talking to fans allows the squad to retain more creative control.

The squad can make informed decisions about how to market and sell the film as they have the relationship with fans. The squad can make insightful changes based on early fan feedback to maintain the artistic value of the film.

Now that we've addressed the most common fears of feedback, let's look at some practical steps for talking to fans.

Start with a spark

Start with a simple idea to explore in fan research interviews.

This idea isn't meant to be a plot description or story summary. It doesn't have to be a high concept or fully formed outline.

Preferably, it's more abstract, ideally grounded in a subject matter with obvious fans.

It's just the spark.

The squad goals from Step 1 can also be the starting point. If these goals don't immediately translate, a few more rounds of Affinity Mapping can help generate more ideas.

For example, our goal for *Solo Woman Traveler* was to showcase the positive representation of a solo woman traveler. All four of the squad members had traveled extensively and two were women with lived experience of solo backpacking.

Apart from a few obvious exceptions, most films about women traveling alone seemed to be thrillers, horrors and cautionary tales. We wanted to test fan interest in a travel story grounded in the real-life nuance of a woman having fun adventures and intense encounters, while growing into a stronger person – without her being assaulted, kidnapped or killed.

We encourage the exploration of diverse subject matter, controversial themes or even topics that have traditionally been considered taboo.

The squad may want to consider any broader ethical questions as well, including:
- × Why do we personally care about this subject?
- × Do any squad members have lived experience with this topic?
- × Are we co-opting or appropriating from other cultures?
- × Is this harmful to marginalized communities or people underrepresented on screen?
- × How can we responsibly dramatize the theme with empathy, care and authenticity?

As this demonstrates, you really don't need much of a spark to get started.

There's also another scenario: the squad wants to work on a preconceived idea that has already been developed into a treatment, story breakdown or even a script.

If this is the case, the story's central theme, subject matter or topic still needs to be broken down into a simple idea for the purpose of research interviews.

Once you have your spark of an idea, it's time to identify some potential fans and conduct research interviews.

Conduct research interviews

Research interviews help validate ideas to ensure they honor the creative ambitions of the squad. They are also crucial to uncovering universal truths that authentically resonate with fans.

Research interviews are a learning exercise that demands the full squad's participation.

As the squad learns about their potential fans, they can draft a fan experience and validate their ideas with tester videos.

Before we get into the nitty gritty of running research interviews, there's a couple of important notes about receiving feedback.

It's essential that feedback is used as an opportunity to learn, rather than justify or defend the squad's decisions.

You'll be doing multiple MSA Cycles so the idea is naturally going to grow and change. There's no need to fiercely protect it from criticism. The squad's job is to listen, interpret and dig into any information that the fans generously share.

All feedback, good or bad, is a precious gift.

If you graciously accept feedback without defensiveness, you'll be rewarded with insights that'll help you make a better film.

And a final word of caution: get feedback from fans, not filmmakers.

It's common practice to pitch ideas to other filmmakers for feedback, but try to resist this impulse. If you share your ideas with filmmakers who haven't been exposed to Lean Filmmaking, they'll likely be resistant to the method and may unintentionally derail your progress.

(There's one exception: if filmmaking is the subject of your film and the intended fans are filmmakers, then sure, go for it.)

Just remember, you don't need peer validation for your idea.

Go directly to fans, they're the ones who'll spend time and money to make your film a success.

Set parameters

Conducting research interviews requires a set of parameters to identify potential fans.

The squad speculates about who early fans will be, then the research interviews confirm, or disqualify, this assertion.

It should be self-evident from the initial idea what type of people the squad should reach out to first. The parameters for research interviews will continue to change as more information is acquired.

When we started researching *Solo Woman Traveler*, our squad started by interviewing women who'd traveled alone overseas in the last five years.

After several interviews, we refined the parameters, adding that they also needed to have traveled solo for longer than two months and spent time backpacking or staying in hostels. These parameters were targeted enough for us to draft the first fan experience.

Recruit potential fans to interview

Once you've established the parameters, the squad needs to recruit potential fans who fit that criteria.

You can start by interviewing friends *but only if* they meet the parameters. It's important to move beyond your own network as soon as possible. (Asking for referrals at the end of every interview will quickly expand your list of contacts.)

It's better to focus on psychographics rather than demographics – for example, solo woman travelers regardless of age, occupation or zip code. You can always add more criteria as you learn from the interviews.

Then comes the tough bit.

You have to email, call, text or direct message people and ask them for an interview.

For example, our squad said, "We're interested in making a film about solo travel. We'd love to hear about your experiences. Do you have thirty minutes to chat about this?"

Sometimes people object, nervous they're not experts or don't know enough about the subject. Reassure them that you're interested in their personal experiences and it's for research purposes only. They probably know way more than they realize – enough to fill thirty minutes – and if they don't, that tells you something useful too.

It's best to do research interviews in person (or an online video call), rather than voice or text only, as it's easier to pick up on important non-verbal cues.

Overall, most people are happy to talk about a topic they're passionate about, as long as you're polite and considerate of their time.

If you're struggling to consistently book interviews, revisit your parameters and try approaching a different cohort of potential fans.

Write interview template

You can get the most value from research interviews by following a consistent structure.

Before the squad starts holding research interviews, they need to write a template with a prepared script and well-thought-out questions.

Following a script in each interview helps to identify patterns and track responses.

Knowing exactly what you're going to say is also a big help if you're nervous about talking to new people. Just smile and stick to the script.

The interview template is divided into three sections: overview, worldview and wrap-up. Each section plays an important role in quickly unearthing useful information.

The overview is a script that's used to explain the interview format and describe the idea.

But keep it vague.

Provide enough context for the conversation to be relevant, without overly priming the person being interviewed.

Priming happens when saying something that unconsciously influences people and guides their behavior. Preparing the interview template in advance helps remove unintentional biases in the language and consider the framing of questions. Let the person being interviewed guide you, not the other way around.

You're trying to get their honest opinions, not what they think you want to hear.

The worldview takes up the bulk of the interview time.

It includes open-ended questions but is flexible enough to dig deeper with clarifying questions like, "Why do you think that happened?", "How did you make that decision?", "What were you thinking leading up to that moment?" or the classic, "That's interesting, how so?"

It's likely not all of the prepared questions will be answered. There's no need to rush through them. It's more important to actively listen, follow the organic flow of the discussion and go beyond the superficial. Allow space for silence after asking a question to prompt deeper answers.

The goal of the worldview is to capture the nuances of the topic, paying special attention to specific phrases and language that the person uses.

Finally, in the wrap-up, ask for referrals and permission to email them updates about the film.

The goal of the wrap-up is to answer final questions, address lingering concerns and get strong referrals.

As an example, this is the first research interview template for *Solo Woman Traveler*. Our initial parameters were women who'd traveled alone overseas in the last five years.

Overview:
Thanks for meeting us. As you know, we're interested in making a film about solo travelers. We'd like to ask you some questions about your personal experiences of traveling alone. Because we haven't made the film yet we're here to learn from you. There are no right or wrong answers. We're interested in your story in your own words. What we talk about today is for our research purposes only. Any information you provide will remain anonymous. Do you have any questions? Let's set a timer for thirty minutes and get started.

Worldview:
If you think back to when you first considered traveling alone, can you talk about your thought process?
Was it always your plan to travel solo?
What research did you do before traveling alone?
What was the conversation like when you told your spouse/friends/parents about your plans to travel solo?
Before leaving, did you imagine what life would be like once you had traveled?
After traveling, how did reality differ from your imagination?
What are the best things about being a solo traveler?
What are the worst things about being a solo traveler?
How has solo traveling made your life better?
Is there a question you wished we'd asked?

Wrap-up:
Our time is up. Do you have any other questions? This has been great; thank you for your time. Would you like to be kept up to date about the progress of the film? [If yes, add to email list] Now that you've gone through this interview process, do you know anyone else who might be able to help us? Can you provide an introduction via email, text or direct messenger? That's it! Thanks again.

After our squad had done multiple interviews, we updated our interview template to reflect what we'd learned.

The overview and wrap-up sections remained the same but the worldview became about specifics, rather than generalities. We added more questions to figure out how to sell and market our film to these fans.

We also refined our parameters to include women who had traveled solo for longer than two months and spent time backpacking or staying in hostels.

This is an example of the worldview in the fourth version of the *Solo Woman Traveler* interview template.

Worldview V4:
What interests you in backpacking rather than other forms of travel?
What was the most important item in your backpack?

What's your best backpacking story, the one you tell people when they ask you about your travels?
What is your worst story, the one you don't ever tell people about backpacking?
Did you watch movies while staying in a hostel?
Why did/didn't you watch movies when staying in a hostel?
What's the most important thing to you about watching movies in a hostel?
Are you interested in seeing a film about the experience of backpacking and staying in hostels?

By thinking about the structure of the interview and writing a template in advance, our squad got tons of detailed information, hilarious anecdotes, real-life personal experiences and powerful insights into the challenges of making a film for this cohort of fans.

Conduct interviews

It's the simple things that help interviews go well. Be on time. Be polite. Be appreciative.

The day prior to the scheduled interview, send a reminder message with any final meeting instructions.

The secret to a good interview is making the participant feel comfortable, that they're in safe hands.

When conducting interviews, it helps to have two squad members present. One person can take the lead reading the script, asking the questions and facilitating the discussion. The other person is responsible for writing detailed notes and being supportive.

Pay close attention to any specific phrases or nuances of language, writing them down word-for-word if possible.

Hopefully the more interviews you do, the more you'll begin to recognize phrases that ring true for your fans, that can be integrated into the idea in an authentic way.

During the interview, it's essential to stay curious and practice active listening.

Thirty minutes flies by very quickly. Don't waste time by injecting your opinion or describing your own experiences.

You're trying to learn – not defend or justify your idea.

Review interviews

When the interview is finished, take a few minutes to write individual notes before getting the whole squad together for a group discussion about key insights.

It's good practice to keep interview notes in a shared location online, so they can easily be referred to again.

Another option is to record the interviews – but there's a drawback to this format. People unconsciously modify their behavior when they're being recorded, making it harder to get the unvarnished truth.

Another downside: when our squad tried recording interviews, we never listened to them again!

Unless the recordings are transcribed, the disadvantages may outweigh the advantages.

We feel it's better to be an active listener and write lots of notes, during and directly after the interview.

After doing multiple interviews, it'll be clear if the parameters need to be adjusted or the questions changed.

The squad should also be on the lookout for ways to improve their process for recruiting participants and conducting interviews.

While doing research interviews for *Solo Woman Traveler*, we streamlined the process to easily interview four people in two hours.

As our squad had four members, we'd break into pairs for the interviews – assigning a facilitator and a note taker for each pair.

We'd hold two in-person interviews every hour. The participants would arrive, we'd take them into separate meeting rooms and each pair would conduct an interview. Then we'd write our individual notes and have a group discussion.

The timing usually worked out as five minutes of getting situated and introductions, thirty minutes for the interview, ten minutes of chitchat with the participant before they left, five minutes to review individual notes, then ten minutes for the whole squad to discuss insights.

Once we got into a steady cadence, we'd schedule interviews for a couple of hours, several nights a week. It was no problem to interview sixteen people in two weeks.

The goal is to complete *at least* ten research interviews.

This will be enough interviews to give an indication of interest in the subject matter, hone fan recruitment tactics, gather basic marketing information and identify recurring themes, specific phrases and common experiences.

While research interviews are fundamental to this step, they're an essential tool that can be deployed whenever more clarity about a topic is required.

Draft a fan experience

In Lean Filmmaking we seek to understand and articulate the fan's experience of a film.

We validate and improve the experience of watching the film so that it connects deeply with our intended fans.

> ### Fan Experience
> The emotions people feel while watching the film and how they describe the story after it's over. The squad's aim is to test, validate and improve the viewing experience until it connects deeply with the intended fans.

The fan experience is the beating heart of the film.

It evokes a powerful reaction in the viewer, like joy, sadness, intrigue, fear or anger. And there may be physical manifestations like laughter, tears and jolting in surprise.

A film with a strong fan experience can be executed in a variety of ways with different plots, characters and styles.

The squad uses insights gleaned from research interviews to write the first draft of a fan experience.

Our first draft of a fan experience for *Solo Woman Traveler* was: be emboldened to travel solo and have globe-trotting adventures.

Our accelerator participants also drafted fan experiences.

Time Apart: feel cathartic despair about the slow disintegration of a long-distance relationship.

Trench: deeply empathize with a victim of abuse who takes drastic measures to survive.

The fan experience can be refined in MSA Cycles. In the first instance just make an educated guess so the squad can start making tester videos.

Make tester videos

Traditionally, filmmakers make short films with slick production values to demonstrate their skills, build a show reel or use as a selling tool for a feature-length version.

This is definitely *not* the purpose of tester videos.

Tester Video

Any kind of lo-fi video content used to validate the fan experience. It's short, easy to produce and has a specific hypothesis to test with fans.

Tester videos are completed in an iterative way using basic Make-Show-Adjust Cycles.

As discussed in Part 1, the work of planning, filming and learning is organized into small continuous cycles. The squads make, show and adjust tester videos (Step 2), then full-film drafts (Step 3) and full-film polishes (Step 4), before converging on the final version of the film.

Keeping tester videos simple reduces resistance to making multiple versions and eases the pain of discarding the ones that aren't working. The squad can take action quickly and learn through doing, rather than wasting time guessing, over-planning or perfecting.

As they are lo-fi, there's less chance of becoming attached to the idea before it's validated, and an increased likelihood the squad will make changes, experiment and improve.

Some examples of tester videos include hand drawn storyboards with a voice over, concept videos with stock footage, simple animatics or basic trailers. As long as the image is in focus and the sound is clear, let your imagination go wild.

In early cycles, when it's just the spark of an idea, one of our favorite tools to explore the fan experience is a Coffee Convo.

A Coffee Convo is a type of tester video that's an acted scenario where two friends have watched an imaginary film and they're chatting over coffee about how it made them feel, as if it's a real film. It needs two actors and a smartphone, and can be shot in one take with the actors improvising the conversation (or performing a script).

As there isn't even a story or plot yet this forces the squad to focus on the fan experience. It's also a great way to incorporate specific language or catchphrases gleaned from research interviews to see if they also connect with other potential fans.

As the cycles progress, the squad can make more sophisticated tester videos, like trailers. But remember to keep the scale small and production values low. They're not meant to be glossy marketing tools (yet). Treat them as experiments to see if the squad can elicit the desired response from fans.

When new to Lean Filmmaking, making tester videos is a low-risk way to practice basic MSA Cycles, before scaling up to feature length.

Tester videos are produced in a condensed, basic version of MSA Cycles due to the short nature of the content. (In Step 3, more structured ceremonies are added to handle the longer duration of full-film drafts.)

Tester videos are lo-fi and simple to produce, keeping MSA Cycles as short as possible.

The time it takes to complete a cycle, and number of cycles required, is determined by the constraints of the squad and the fan feedback they receive. But it's easier to maintain a consistent cadence if each cycle is the same length.

If the work doesn't fit into the agreed cadence, you're probably trying to do too much.

Improving production values isn't an accurate indication of progress. Instead, focus on testing the hypotheses in lo-fi ways.

For *Solo Woman Traveler*, our cadence for tester videos was one MSA Cycle per week.

As all the squad members had day jobs, we met two nights a week for three hours and did a few hours of extra administration. We made the tester video in one night and the other night we collected and analyzed fan feedback. To efficiently use our limited time, we recruited fans and scheduled interviews throughout the week.

Another example of a different cadence for tester videos is four MSA Cycles in a weekend.

As part of the accelerator, the squads for *Time Apart* and *Trench* made four versions of a short concept video in two days using a similar structure to the Filmmakathon.

These are the key actions in each basic MSA Cycle:

Make
- × Determine test
- × Plan production
- × Make tester video

Show
- × Recruit fans
- × Show tester video
- × Collect fan feedback

Adjust
- × Analyze fan feedback
- × Adjust fan experience
- × Improve squad workflow

Make

The first stage in the cycle is Make. It includes all the work required to complete a tester video.

The squad identifies a hypothesis to test and determines what will be considered a success or failure. When in doubt, do the easiest test first.

After drafting our fan experience for *Solo Woman Traveler*, we made three different Coffee Convos to test the insights gained through research interviews. Our hypothesis was that we could accurately reflect the positive feelings evoked by traveling alone as a woman by using specific language and universal experiences.

We would consider the test a success if 75% of the respondents agreed with our hypothesis.

The squad has a short planning meeting to organize any production requirements. Then the squad makes the tester video.

After some practice, our squad could make tester videos for *Solo Woman Traveler* in a few hours. That's everything from deciding the hypothesis to test, to shooting and editing. This gave us incredible flexibility to quickly test our ideas, without worrying about perfection or fancy production values.

Show

The second stage in the cycle is Show. It includes all the work to find fans, screen the tester video and collect feedback.

During this stage the squad needs to actively recruit new fans.

Potential fans can come from a variety of sources. Referrals from research interviews are a starting point. Also pay attention to any events, conferences, festivals, businesses, cafes, meetups, social media platforms and websites where your fans congregate.

You're looking for genuine connections. Be transparent, considerate and authentic. Not creepy or spammy.

For example, our potential fans for *Solo Woman Traveler* were always traveling and meeting lots of new people, which gave us heaps of quality referrals. But in addition, we asked the organizers of meetups dedicated to women travelers for permission to speak at their events about our film. We also spoke to people who worked at hostels and put up flyers on their notice boards.

At this stage, it's also helpful to use a simple spreadsheet or database to keep track of the people you've interviewed, their feedback and contact details.

The most important marketing tool to start building a community is an email list. The squad can start collecting email addresses (with permission) and sending regular updates. There are lots of free email marketing services that make this easy to manage.

Then you need to show the tester video to these fans, either in person or online, and collect their feedback.

There are many ways to collect feedback, including interviews, surveys and analyzing data from online viewing. Each method has different benefits.

In the first instance, we recommend in-person feedback as there's a lot to learn from body language and non-verbal communication. Seeing someone laugh, or look confused, tells you as much as what they say verbally.

We gather feedback by conducting reaction interviews.

Reaction interviews have a similar overview and wrap-up as research interviews, but in the worldview section, a tester video is shown for immediate feedback. (All of the other instructions for conducting interviews still apply.)

Reaction interviews are a way to ascertain if the hypothesis being tested has succeeded or failed. As tester videos are short, they can be screened during the interview to gauge the impact on the participant. Then the squad can ask follow-up questions to dig deeper into their responses.

As an example, this is the reaction interview template for *Solo Woman Traveler*.

Overview:
Thanks for meeting us. We're interested in making a film about solo travelers. We'd like to ask you some questions about your personal experiences of traveling alone. We'll also show you a short video to get your feedback. Because we haven't made the film yet we're here to learn from you. There are no right or wrong answers. We're interested in your story in your own words. What we talk about today is for our research purposes only. Any information you provide will remain anonymous. Do you have any questions? Let's set a timer for thirty minutes and get started.

Worldview:
What interests you in backpacking rather than other forms of travel?
Are you interested in seeing a film about the experience of backpacking and staying in hostels? We're going to show you a short video now and we'll talk about it afterwards.

[Screen tester video]
How did that make you feel?
What was your favorite part?
What was your least favorite part?
Based just on this short video, what do you think this film is about?
Does it make you want to watch the whole film?
Would you recommend this to a friend who's also interested in travel?
Is there anything we haven't covered that you think is important for us to know about solo traveling?

Wrap-up:
Our time is up. Do you have any other questions? This has been great; thank you for your time. Would you like to be kept up to date about the progress of the film? [If yes, add to email list] Now that you've gone through this interview process, do you know anyone else who might be able to help us? Can you provide an introduction via email, text or direct messenger? That's it! Thanks again.

It's not always possible to do in-person interviews and sometimes it's more practical to use an online survey or short questionnaire. If the squad has a large list of people who've already participated in research interviews, then a short survey with a link to view the tester video online is an easy way to get more feedback.

For *Solo Woman Traveler*, we used this template to send out tester videos to fans:

> Based on your feedback we've made a short video. Please watch it here [insert link] and answer these questions by [insert deadline].
> What do you think this film is about?
> Which part did you like the most?
> Which part did you like the least?
> How did it make you feel?
> Does this make you want to watch the whole film?
> Would you recommend this film to a friend?

The additional advantage for online viewing is that it can provide more data like email open rate, click-through rate, number of shares and video watch time.

After interviews and surveys, organize the fan feedback in a central place ready for the next stage.

Adjust

The third stage of the cycle is Adjust. It includes analyzing the fan feedback, refining the fan experience and discussing squad learnings.

The squad analyzes the fan feedback, determines if the test has succeeded or failed and considers new hypotheses to test in the next cycle.

This is also a good time for the squad to discuss what they learned about working together in this cycle and how their workflow can be improved.

Repeat

Then do it all again. Keep repeating the cycle of Make-Show-Adjust until the squad has tested the idea and validated the fan experience.

In our hypothetical *Solo Woman Traveler*, the squad did six basic MSA Cycles, making two Coffee Convos and four trailers.

The squad conducted eight reaction interviews and twenty online surveys for each Coffee Convo, then another sixteen reaction interviews and thirty online surveys for the trailers. On average, at least 60% of the participants were new in each cycle. It was a thrill every time one of these women exclaimed, "That's *exactly* how it feels!". We consistently signed up 80% of the participants to our email list and 40% referred other women for us to interview.

We moved on from Coffee Convos to making simple trailers after hitting our success rate of 75% of the participants agreeing that we accurately reflected the positive feelings evoked by traveling alone as a woman.

We wanted to test different genres to gauge the reaction of our potential fans. Our first two trailers were aspirational dramas but they received very mixed reactions. As a squad, we also struggled to connect with the genre and feared it would be tough to deliver a globe-trotting drama within our constraints.

For the third trailer, we lost sight of our fan experience. It was a thriller. Needless to say, it got resounding negative feedback.

We took a step back and went though all of the feedback. We realized that if we wanted to target women currently backpacking alone (not just those who had solo traveled in the past) there were interesting opportunities.

From our interviews, we knew that backpackers primarily spend their money on accommodation, excursions, partying and food – not movies. In fact, staying in a hostel made it easy to swap film files with other travelers, share streaming services or just watch whatever was available in the communal recreation room.

We started to think about how to take advantage of this situation. Rather than just guess, we did some quick research by calling ten hostels to ask the managers what movie facilities they offered customers. It was time well spent!

We learned that all of the hostels had a common room with a large TV and facilities to play DVDs or stream movies. Only 30% actively encouraged or programmed movie nights but several others said they were always looking for ideas to entertain guests, especially those with onsite bars.

We decided to make a film that directly tapped into the backpacker experience, that could be watched multiple times and enjoyed with a noisy crowd of people. We wanted a film where the more you watched it, the better the in-jokes and one-liners became. Hopefully word-of-mouth about the film would organically promote the film as backpackers shared it while traveling from place to place, creating a grassroots following.

We also thought selling movie night packages directly to hostel managers meant we wouldn't have to only rely on cash-strapped travelers to purchase the film.

We tested our theory with a new trailer: a zombie action-comedy set inside a hostel under attack by the undead. Our main character is a kick-ass solo woman backpacker who drinks hard, breaks hearts and kills zombies. She discovers that being drunk makes people "invisible" to the zombies. Sober up, you die. But saving the day with strength, humor and compassion, while wasted, is its own special challenge.

This felt like a *big* pivot.

There's no way our squad would've come up with this idea without research interviews and tester videos.

We adjusted the fan experience for *Solo Woman Traveler* to: delight in relatable misadventures, hostel in-jokes and the gratification of being a solo woman backpacker.

You're done with this step when...

You've got an idea for a feature film that's been endorsed by fans through research interviews.

You've validated a fan experience with tester videos, consistently eliciting the intended emotional response.

You've started a marketing email list and can recruit new fans in a sustainable way.

As a squad, you've become proficient at conducting

interviews, receiving feedback and running basic MSA Cycles.

The final part of this step is to determine how the next step will be resourced.

In the next step, the squad will produce full-length film drafts but they'll be lo-fi, as the goal is to validate the story before adding any production values.

We've demonstrated it's possible to gain valuable insights without investing much cash. Even though it's tempting to spend money, the most important resource is still time.

Confirm everyone's commitment to the project with a Go/No Go Meeting and revisit the work schedule.

If you can complete the below checklist, and understand the tools, you're ready to move on to the next step.

Step 2 Checklist
- × Find the spark of an idea
- × Conduct research interviews
- × Write draft fan experience
- × Create tester videos in basic MSA Cycles
- × Start a simple fan database and email list
- × Set date for next Go/No Go Meeting
- × Commit to work schedule for the next step

Step 2 Tools
- × Research interviews
- × Basic Make-Show-Adjust Cycles
- × Reaction interviews

Step 3: Develop Drafts

It's crucial to find a connection between a story worth telling and the fans who want to see it.

The third step in the Lean Filmmaking method is to develop full-film drafts until the story has proven its appeal to fans.

As well as the benefits gained from putting the story before production values, there are other advantages to developing drafts, including:
- × Exploiting lo-fi techniques to test the entire film
- × Visually representing the film with a Story Scaffold
- × Using fan experience improvements to validate the story
- × Increasing success rate by adding ceremonies to MSA Cycles

You've done research interviews, drafted the fan experience and validated your idea with tester videos, but in this step you'll shift to seeing the entire story through the eyes of fans by developing full-film drafts.

The Lean Filmmaking Method

Step 1: Form Squad

   Validate: Squad goals

↓

Step 2: Discover Fans

   Validate: Fan experience
      ✘ Tester videos
      ✘ Reaction interviews

↓

Step 3: Develop Drafts

Validate: Story–Fan Fit
    ✘ Full-film drafts
    ✘ Free fan screenings
    ✘ Story improvements

↓

Step 4: Produce Polishes

   Validate: Production–Fan Fit
      ✘ Full-film polishes
      ✘ Paid fan screenings
      ✘ Production improvements

↓

Step 5: Launch Film

   Validate: Distribution strategy

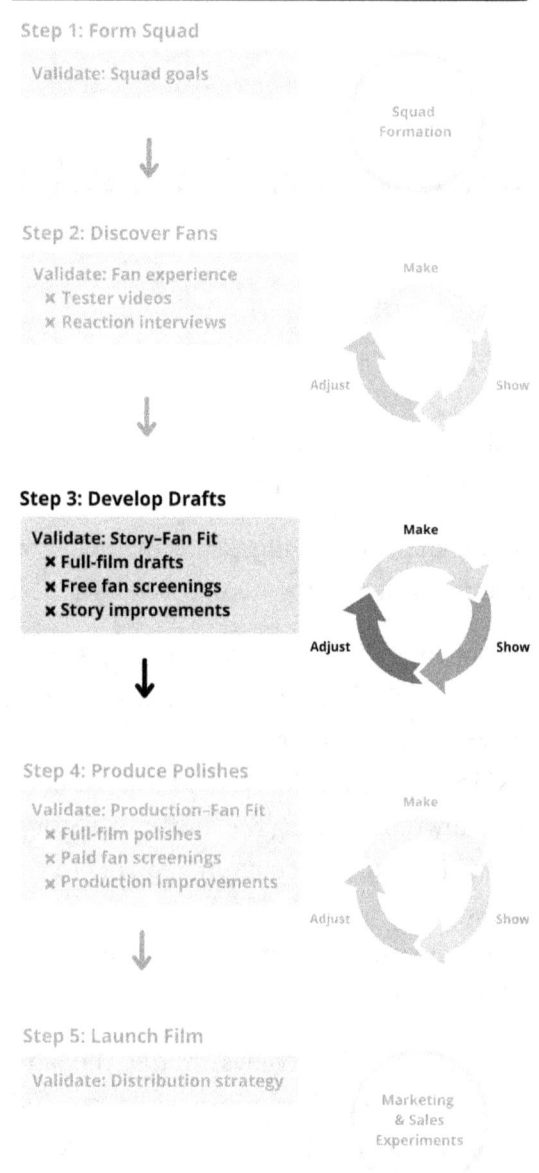

Full-film Drafts
Lo-fi versions of the entire film created in Make-Show-Adjust Cycles, with the aim of continuously improving the story, exploring the fan experience and ultimately finding Story–Fan Fit.

It's time to bring the story to life.

In a lo-fi way.

And we mean *lo-fi*.

Lower than that, like, really lo-fi.

We're confident you'll be able to execute the technical aspects of film production, but before wasting time, money and energy on crafting the aesthetics, let's make sure you have a story worth telling.

At this stage, you're still learning about the story and can't possibly plan how/when/where to shoot the final version of the film. Glossy production values, if required, will be added in the next step; for now, just get cozy with the notion of raw, rough and unpolished.

People assume that most of the creative part of filmmaking happens during production. It's easy to mistake this for the real work of filmmaking.

But most of the time, that's not the case.

The massive financial burden, crushing long hours, department rivalries and unrelenting pressure to get the perfect take before going into overtime or losing the light don't make traditional film shoots conducive to creativity at all.

The stress of inevitable setbacks that delay production can choke collaboration and hamper honest communication, the very things that foster creativity.

It doesn't have to be like this.

But it does require completely rethinking how to shoot films.

We've made this possible by delivering full-film drafts and testing assumptions through standard Make-Show-Adjust Cycles.

Ceremonies empower the squad

The main difference (apart from the length) between a basic cycle used to make tester videos and a standard Make-Show-Adjust Cycle is the inclusion of formal ceremonies.

In Lean Filmmaking, ceremonies are important events during the standard MSA Cycle that facilitate the successful delivery of a full film, either a draft or polish.

Ceremonies empower the squad by reinforcing collaboration, strengthening communication and continuously improving the squad's workflow. Each ceremony has a different purpose, but together they provide a framework that encourages transparency and teamwork.

All squad members participate in these ceremonies.

There are four ceremonies in each cycle: cycle planning, standups, fan experience improvement review and squad retrospective.

Cycle Planning
Held at the beginning of the Make stage. The squad commits to the amount of work as an achievable goal for the cycle. The squad chooses the appropriate number of fan experience improvements to be executed in the cycle and breaks them into individual tasks.

Standups
Happen during the Make stage when the squad meets for quick status updates. They're short catch-ups to communicate what tasks everyone is doing and troubleshoot issues that may hinder the completion of the work.

Fan Experience Improvement Review
Happens at the start of the Adjust stage. The squad decides which fan experience improvements succeeded or failed, based on feedback gathered in the cycle. Fan experience improvements are added, removed, adjusted and prioritized on the Story Scaffold backlog.

Squad Retrospective

Held at the end of the Adjust stage. The squad reflects on their workflow, making improvements for future cycles. Most commonly, everyone answers three questions about the cycle: what worked, what didn't work, and what was confusing.

Each of these ceremonies is discussed more in running a full-film draft MSA Cycle, but before the squad can begin, let's introduce overlapping activities, just-in-time production, Story Scaffolds and fan experience improvements.

Restructure work by overlapping activities

We've restructured the work involved in making a film: instead of being completed in a linear fashion, many of the activities will overlap. This is a collaborative way to improve output and efficiently distribute the workload between squad members.

To give a practical example, for a squad of six who've decided their primary roles are a writer, director, shooter, editor and two actors, this work could be allocated at the same time:

- × The writer is writing story beats, action or dialogue for the next scene
- × The director and actors are rehearsing the current scene
- × The shooter is finding locations and setting up shots for the current scene
- × The editor is editing the previous scene

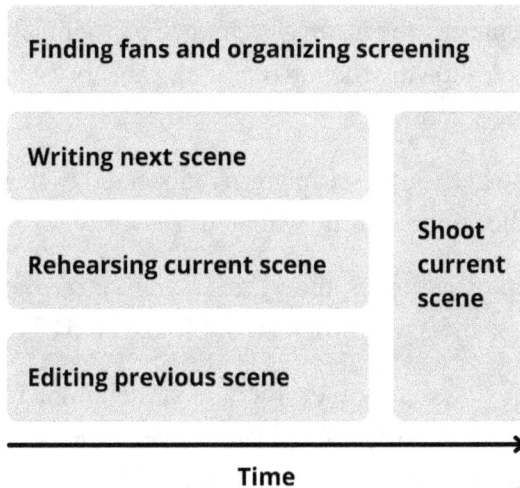

The squad comes together at predetermined times to view the edit of the previous scene, shoot the current scene and discuss the tasks for the next scene, before separating again to repeat the process.

This is done concurrently, in real time, making it easy to quickly adjust performance, style, pacing and most importantly, story.

The actors can ask the editor why a scene was cut in a certain way, then adapt their performance when shooting the next scene.

The writer can see how much detail the actors need to perform a scene, providing them with only the essentials in the next scene.

The cinematographer can get character insights from the writer, allowing them to enhance the story with appropriate shots.

Everyone in the squad can give feedback on each scene within the context of the whole film.

Overlapping activities allow the squad to interrogate every task and assess when (or if) it needs to be done.

If the squad has only a few members, then implementing overlapping activities will obviously be harder – but there's a positive trade-off with other time-saving benefits, like a reduction in documentation and fewer chances for miscommunication.

For example, if the same person is directing, shooting and editing, they can design the scene in a way that will make all of those activities easier and with less chance of the desired execution being lost in translation.

Overlapping activities can also be a valuable tool in all stages, not just Make. During the Show and Adjust stages, different squad members can be interviewing fans, organizing screenings, collating feedback or producing marketing materials.

The skills and talents of each squad member will become apparent through doing multiple MSA Cycles. The squad retrospective provides an opportunity to review how overlapping activities are working and where they can be improved in future cycles.

Delay decisions with just-in-time production

The goal of just-in-time production is to make decisions as close to the act of doing the work as possible.

Instead of deciding every last detail upfront, the planning is purposely kept minimal.

Sparse, even.

Ideally, production decisions are delayed until the last responsible time.

In Lean Filmmaking, we reduce investment in production values until the story has been validated. This is an important distinction as it's the opposite of traditional filmmaking practices, where most of the big financial decisions are based on an untested script.

Remarkably, you don't need very high production values to test the story with your initial fans. We've received valuable feedback from storyboards with hand-drawn stick-figures.

Our focus is on exploring the essence of the scene, dramatizing the central conflict, moving the plot forward and revealing character – all from a story perspective.

Any ancillary information like specific locations, props, set design or costumes are excluded for now, leaving out everything that's not essential.

The squad uses the minimum effort required to construct a scene, using lo-fi representations whenever possible.

Can props be made from cardboard? Can the action take place in a parked, rather than moving, vehicle? Can the actors wear the same costume in every scene?

The descriptive scene headings used in scripts – day or night, interior or exterior – don't matter, as they can just be added as temporary captions on screen to give an indication of the intended settings.

There's no point wasting time finding "perfect" locations until the story has been validated by fans.

For example, as locations aren't essential, shooting in full-film drafts can take place in any environment that's convenient (and free!). The squad can also take advantage of whatever the weather happens to be at the time of the shoot. If it's raining, getting some dramatic shots outside could be beneficial but if the additional effort isn't worth it, then shoot indoors.

"We found a warehouse and shot an entire draft version at this location in just two days. It was all about getting the story up, seeing how it walked and talked." —Paul Anthony Nelson, producer *Trench*

Gradually, improvements are added to full-film drafts as they're completed in MSA Cycles, but it's always important to ask: does this decision need to be made right now?

Construct the Story Scaffold

We've already talked about the limitations of scripts but now is a good time to revisit their role within the context of standard MSA Cycles.

In Part 1: Core Values, we focused on the benefits of starting with a story, not a script. This doesn't mean that dialogue, scenes or eventually even a script won't be written, it's just not the starting point. A script isn't the only way to move forward with production.

In Part 2: Step 1, we highlighted the importance of forming a squad, before writing a script. Writing is still a core skill required for a well-balanced squad but it's an activity that's done in a collaborative way.

In this step, we validate our assumptions about the story with fans as early as possible.

Traditional filmmaking places a great deal of faith in scripts. This false sense of security encourages people to make big irreversible decisions before validating the assumptions scattered on every page.

Assumptions about who the fans are for the film.

Assumptions about how high production values need to be to satisfy these fans.

Assumptions about casting, locations, special effects, music and a thousand other moving parts that make up a film.

And if these assumptions are wrong, it costs us dearly.

It's difficult to unearth these assumptions when the only tool is a script.

A script isn't the final product that's consumed by an audience, like a book, song or even a painting hanging on a gallery wall.

It's a technical document used as a proxy for the eventual film. It's not effective for fans to give feedback on a script because everything changes when it's translated into a film.

The faster full-film drafts are made, the sooner complex story challenges (easily overlooked in a script) can be solved and assumptions can be validated.

With all of this in mind, articulating a story can take on many forms.

Nothing has to be written in entirety from beginning to end. Scenes and sequences are jotted down as required. Dialogue is improvised by actors or quickly scribbled by the writer.

Of course, it's still useful to conceptualize the story, keep track of development and provide a visual reference for production. But this can be an accumulation of sticky notes, index cards, drawings, photos, diagrams and storyboards, rather than long pages of written description.

Lean Filmmaking introduces two new tools that work hand-in-hand to replace the traditional script format during standard MSA Cycles: the Story Scaffold and fan experience improvements.

Story Scaffold

An ephemeral physical or digital representation, illustrating the current version of the entire story and assisting the squad in visualizing the film's structure to achieve the desired fan experience.

Fan Experience Improvements

Incremental changes, executed in MSA Cycles, to test if the fan experience can be improved by their inclusion. They are self-contained, verifiable and small enough to be completed in one cycle.

First, let's talk about the Story Scaffold in a little more detail.

The Story Scaffold is a visual representation of the current story and future fan experience improvements, made up of three sections.

The top section is simple: at the top of the Story Scaffold is the current version of the fan experience. This acts as a touchstone for the squad as they develop drafts.

The middle section has two parts. The first part is the current fan experience improvements that are to be executed in the cycle. The second part is the breakdown of the current story, represented by diagrams, photos, index notes, sticky notes and/or storyboards.

The bottom section is the Story Scaffold backlog. This is a placeholder for new fan experience improvements that have been prioritized, ready for execution in future cycles.

Fan experience

Fan experience improvements (current cycle)

Improve film by _____
so fans feel _____

Improve film by _____
so fans feel _____

Storyboard, image,
reference material, etc

[Photo]   [Photo]

Storyboard, image,
reference material, etc

Sticky note

Sticky note

Sticky note

Storyboard, image,
reference material, etc

Sticky note   Sticky note   Sticky note

Sticky note   Sticky note   Sticky note

Sticky note   Sticky note   Sticky note

Backlog

Improve film by _____
so fans feel _____

Improve film by _____
so fans feel _____

Improve film by _____
so fans feel _____

Improve film by _____
so fans feel _____

Improve film by _____
so fans feel _____

Improve film by _____
so fans feel _____

Improve film by _____
so fans feel _____

Improve film by _____
so fans feel _____

A Story Scaffold isn't meant to be high-fidelity. As always, lo-fi is better. It's a tool to help everyone in the squad move forward in the same direction.

Assume that everything on the Story Scaffold will be moved, replaced or discarded as the film takes shape through the cycles. The scaffolding is a temporary support structure that's removed when the film can stand on its own.

Ideally, the Story Scaffold is displayed on a physical wall in a space where the squad can also hold their ceremonies. A physical location makes it easier to envisage the film as a whole, make changes quickly and facilitate easier discussions.

But if squad members are working remotely, the Story Scaffold can be virtual, using digital tools available online. To avoid going back to a written representation of the film, it's best to use drawing tools to capture ideas.

All squad members can suggest amendments to the Story Scaffold, but it should be the responsibility of one person to organize this tool – normally the writer.

After the squad selects the fan experience improvements to be executed on the next cycle, the writer amends the Story Scaffold, and as the work is done, they update it to reflect the current state of the story. The writer also manages the Story Scaffold backlog and facilitates the fan experience improvement review.

We've talked broadly about fan experience improvements but let's get into the specifics.

They are clear, easily describable changes to the film, intended to improve the fan experience.

Fan experience improvements have the following characteristics:
- × Self-contained – can be prioritized independently
- × Feasible – can be executed in a single cycle
- × Verifiable – can be tested to confirm/refute the expected result

Each individual fan experience improvement is written on an index card in this format: Improve the film by [insert fan experience improvement] so fans feel [insert emotion].

Here are some examples of fan experience improvements:
- × Improve the film by increasing the conflict between the external environment and the character's goals with life and death stakes so the fans feel edge-of-their-seat tension
- × Improve the film by incorporating a naturalistic style so fans feel empathy, like they're walking in the shoes of relatable real people
- × Improve the film by creating a destructive love triangle so fans feel anguish when the primary relationship breaks down
- × Improve the film by adding sparks of humor to illuminate the dark subject matter so fans feel sharp relief at unexpected moments

Fan experience improvements can be executed in multiple ways. The breakdown of improvements into specific tasks happens during the cycle planning ceremony.

For example, the improvement about adding sparks of humor could be executed by giving a character sarcastic dialogue, adding a voice over of a character's ironic inner monologue, having scenes with surprising physical comedy, changing the soundtrack or using unusual props that juxtapose with the seriousness of a scene.

There are many tools at the squad's disposal to make improvements, including the basics of changing locations, subplots, pacing, tone, camera movements, performance, lighting, sound effects, music...the list goes on.

It's up to the squad to determine the specific tasks for improvements, and tests to run, during the Make stage.

For now, once all of the improvements are written, they're added to the backlog then moved to the current Story Scaffold when they're ready to be tested.

During the cycle, especially the Show and Adjust stages, all of the squad members will probably have lots of new ideas. These can be captured as fan experience improvements and added to the Story Scaffold backlog at any time, ready for a group discussion in the next fan experience improvement review.

Install the first Story Scaffold

Before starting standard MSA Cycles, the squad needs to create the initial Story Scaffold.

And it's essential to explore the story at its intended length. It's a feature, not a short film. The first version of the Story Scaffold needs to have enough character development, plot and conflict to make this longer duration possible.

There's little point in spending time, money and energy making the first ten minutes "perfect" before moving onto the rest of the film, because when another hour is added, it causes a ripple effect, changing the entire structure of the story.

A quick aside: we're obviously non-traditionalists. We don't care about your film's duration *as long as* it's validated by fans. And if you're self-distributing, make up your own rules! Traditional distribution adheres to conventional technical standards, including duration. Most festivals and distributors expect a feature film length to be seventy minutes (at the minimum), but more commonly it's ninety-plus minutes.

The whole squad creates the initial Story Scaffold, ready for the first MSA Cycle. This may take several hours or several days.

In the first instance, the writer(s) will collaborate with the other squad members, using their preferred process to sketch out a high-level outline of the story. The writer(s) might even prepare a treatment or concept document to present to the squad.

The high-level story outline could include things like:
- A three-act structure, with turning points and act breaks
- Important scenes or sequences that progress the plot
- Introduction of key characters
- Points of dramatic conflict
- Recurring themes or metaphors

We're not prescriptive about what kind of story structure the squad uses.

As a great place to start filling out the story, we personally like using the three-act structure with a setup, inciting incident, second act break, midpoint, third act break, climax and resolution.

Affinity Mapping is another excellent tool to help the squad flesh out the story.

And remember, the story is represented by a combination of diagrams, photos, index cards, sticky notes and storyboards, rather than long pages of written descriptions or dialogue.

"To turn the idea into a scene-by-scene outline we put the film's basic structure, with all the acts and turning points, up on a whiteboard and used sticky notes to fill the story out." —Ric Forster, writer/director *Time Apart*

If you're using the Lean Filmmaking method to produce a completed script, now is the time to translate that document into a Story Scaffold. The Story Scaffold is designed to quickly make changes, easily visualize the overall story and provide transparency to the whole squad. This is difficult to achieve with a traditional script.

(We're not saying it's *impossible* to shoot a full-film draft using a script, but it requires a high degree of communication and a new draft to be written for each cycle.)

Remember, the Story Scaffold is never perfect or finished.

It's a temporary support structure, not set in stone.

It's a tool to record ideas and an ephemeral representation of the story as it stands for now.

A special note about the very first standard MSA Cycle: it's a little different to other cycles.

There won't be any fan experience improvements to prioritize and test yet – translating the Story Scaffold into a film version is the goal for the first cycle.

It's also highly likely this first full-film draft will also be the shortest, and that's fine. The squad can gradually work up to longer durations in future cycles.

"What's great about the first cycle is it gets momentum going, and you realize that perhaps there are fewer barriers than you imagined." —Melanie Rowland, producer *Time Apart*

Now the squad is ready to start standard MSA Cycles, using their creativity, talent and skills to interpret the Story Scaffold into a full-film draft.

Run full-film draft Make-Show-Adjust Cycles

It's time to take the lessons learned from running basic MSA Cycles and apply them to full-film drafts.

Full-film drafts are completed in an iterative way using standard MSA Cycles. All squad members are involved in every stage. As the story develops, the squad evaluates ways to improve the fan experience, with a goal of achieving Story–Fan Fit.

> ### Story–Fan Fit
> A strong connection between a story worth telling and the fans who want to see it. This is achieved by using Make-Show-Adjust Cycles to develop full-film drafts that validate the story with fans.

As discussed in Part 1, the work of planning, filming and learning is organized into small continuous cycles. The squads make, show and adjust tester videos (Step 2), then full-film drafts (Step 3) and full-film polishes (Step 4), before converging on the final version of the film.

These are the key actions, including ceremonies, in each standard MSA Cycle:

Make
- × Cycle planning
- × Make full-film draft
- × Standups

Show
- × Recruit fans
- × Show full-film draft
- × Collect fan feedback

Adjust
- × Analyze fan feedback
- × Fan experience improvement review
- × Squad retrospective

Like with tester videos, the time each cycle takes to complete and the number of cycles required is determined by the constraints of the squad and the fan feedback they receive.

There's no perfect cycle length but it's easier to maintain a consistent cadence if the duration of each cycle is the same.

We recommend weekly or fortnightly cycles if the squad is working full time on the project, but we've experimented with a variety of different cadences, including monthly cycles when the squad is making the film around day jobs.

For *Solo Woman Traveler*, our cadence for full-film drafts was one MSA Cycle every five weeks.

As part of the accelerator, the squads for *Time Apart* and *Trench* completed three full-film draft MSA Cycles in just over three months, around their day jobs. The duration of the stages within each cycle was two to three weeks for make, one week for show and one week for adjust.

"We finished rehearsing, shooting and editing our first draft in three weeks. That's going from a five-page outline to a feature-length version. We'd pick a scene and just do it. We let go of being perfect."
—Ric Forster, writer/director *Time Apart*

"By shooting a bare-bones draft version of the film in only two days, then showing that to a potential audience for feedback, we gleaned incredible insights that would never have occurred to us otherwise."
—Paul Anthony Nelson, producer *Trench*

In principle, shorter cycles are better. They build momentum and quickly increase the speed of learning.

If cycles get too long, the squad is probably adding unnecessary production values or attempting to execute more fan experience improvements than realistically possible.

Fan experience improvements that can validate the largest elements of the story are done as a priority.

It's a good rule of thumb to test the riskiest assumptions first, then work your way through to the ones with the least consequences.

A high-risk assumption is something that impacts the success of the whole film – for example, that the main location must be an exotic island, a specific special effect is required to sell the concept, or it's set in another time period.

It's important to test the story to see if it can, or can't, stand on its own without high-risk elements.

Standard MSA Cycles may feel labor-intensive at first while the squad learns how to navigate this new way of working. As the squad's confidence grows, the mechanics of running cycles will become second nature, freeing up more energy to focus on creativity.

Make

The first stage in the cycle is Make. It includes all of the work required to complete a full-film draft like writing, acting, shooting, directing and editing.

Implementing overlapping activities and just-in-time production ensures a full-film draft can be completed in each cycle.

There are two ceremonies that take place in the Make stage: cycle planning and standups.

Cycle planning is held at the beginning of the Make stage.

First, the squad commits to the amount of work as an achievable goal for the cycle, decides which fan experience improvements from the Story Scaffold backlog to execute and designs the tests that will confirm/refute the improvement.

(After the first cycle, the improvements in the Story Scaffold backlog have already been organized and prioritized during the fan experience improvement review, held in the Adjust stage of the last cycle.)

Then the squad breaks down the improvements and tests into discrete tasks to be executed in the current cycle.

In the first cycle, the goal of translating the Story Scaffold into a full-film draft can be divided into discrete tasks as well.

The squad member responsible for each task is decided as the cycle progresses.

When deciding tasks, it's worth asking questions like:
- × How can the skills of the squad be put to the best use today?
- × What roadblocks could get in the way of completing this task?
- × Can this task be simplified to achieve the same goal?
- × Can this task be completely avoided?
- × Is there a more lo-fi way to execute this task?

We've found that a Kanban Board is an excellent tool to organize the tasks. This helps the squad visualize the work, limit the amount of work in progress and track the workflow in a transparent way.

Just-in-time production also plays an important role in cycle planning. If the squad has to decide between two similar tasks, or two different ways to achieve a similar objective, they should choose to try the easiest first. Postpone as many production decisions as possible.

Once the tasks are listed, cycle planning is complete and the squad can start shooting and editing the full-film draft.

To improve communication, accountability and transparency through the Make stage, the squad does regular standups. These quick catch-ups ensure everyone knows what's happening and can troubleshoot issues that may hinder the completion of the work.

And if everyone is literally standing up, it keeps the meeting from running too long.

There are many ways to run standups but it can be as simple as each squad member briefly stating what they're working on and anything that may slow or stop their progress. If there's a clear, easy solution for an issue then it can be addressed immediately, but if it requires more discussion, it can be taken offline for a deeper dive into the problem.

It can also be done by walking through the Kanban Board to keep the discussion framed around the work in progress.

The squad may decide to set a regular time for standups. For example, if the squad is working on the project full time, they could agree to all meet at 10am to talk about the next twenty-four hours. If it's a side-project, the squad could do a standup at the beginning of their allocated work time.

At the end of the standup, the squad members continue working on their tasks.

This is when overlapping activities give the squad a huge advantage.

For example, the first task of the writer is to update the Story Scaffold, reflecting the changes from new fan experience improvements. The cinematographer may start scouting locations. The director can start rehearsing with the actors. All of these activities can happen at the same time.

Strict creative constraints are always very useful and artificial limitations help keep the drafts lo-fi, especially for the first few cycles.

Some of our favorite tricks include using only wide shots, having a predetermined number of shots or only shooting one take.

"We decided to shoot the whole film handheld and use natural light as much as possible." —Ric Forster, writer/director Time Apart

It's also possible for full-film drafts to be a raw combination of storyboards, voice over, stock footage, animatic sequences and improvised scenes shot in a makeshift location, with captions to give an indication of the intended setting.

Another practical constraint is a strict deadline for feedback, for example, by scheduling a fan screening shortly after completing the Make stage.

It's important to note: finding fans is an ongoing task that can be done at any time, but the Make stage isn't the time to get any fan feedback. The squad needs to concentrate on making, without outside judgement.

The squad gets fan feedback in the Show stage and reviews it in the Adjust stage.

The Make stage is for creating, playing and experimenting.

Show

The second stage in the cycle is Show. It includes showing the full-film draft and collecting feedback from fans. This is the time to recruit more fans (if the squad hasn't already done so in the Make stage).

The squad shows their full-film draft to fans, getting feedback to determine if the fan experience improvements implemented in the cycle resonated in the intended way.

At the moment, the most important marketing tool is still the email list.

It's still too early for other marketing tactics, like social media or publicity, right now.

But as getting feedback in this step is done through free full-film draft screenings, some extra promotional materials, like a poster and trailer, may be needed to entice people to attend these events.

The squad can allocate time at the beginning of the Show stage to design a poster and make a lo-fi trailer that reflects the full-film draft.

We suggest that free fan screenings are informal, small and lo-fi, just like the draft of the film.

Preferably, use a free venue, as this will be the first of many screenings.

The squad can host this event anywhere that has a screen, like a company boardroom, co-working space or even in your living room. (Of course, consider the privacy and security implications about hosting in your own home; maybe use this just for known contacts.)

Once the venue is secured, squad members can invite fans to a screening through their personal email, messaging apps and social media accounts.

Ideally, you'll have between four to ten people attend the screening. You don't need large numbers to get useful feedback for the next cycle. It's better to have smaller screenings, more often, rather than one large screening.

After the squad screens the full-film draft, they facilitate a group feedback session, called a fan review. The goal is to see if improvements executed in the cycle succeeded – or failed – to improve the fan experience.

If there are fewer than six people, the fan review can be done together as one group – but more people than that can get unwieldy. If that's the case, split into several smaller groups with different squad members facilitating each one.

The facilitator draws a symbol on three sticky notes to represent each category of reflection and puts them up on a wall:
- ★ What was your favorite part?
- ♥ How did it make you feel?
- ? What was confusing?

Set a timer for three minutes. Everyone silently writes sticky notes with their feedback about these categories.

Each person then takes turns putting their sticky notes up on the wall under the appropriate category, briefly describing each one without interruption from anyone else. Any similar ideas can be grouped together.

When all the sticky notes are up, a squad member facilitates a discussion about the feedback. The facilitator may also decide to choose some specific feedback to use as a starting point for another round to dive deeper and get more insights.

It's also helpful to have a survey prepared to be filled out before the fans leave the screening, including opt-in permission for the email list, suggested referrals and request for a reaction interview (to be done online or in person).

After the attendees leave, the squad can make notes about the feedback gathered during the fan review.

"There's a massive difference between getting feedback on a script and getting feedback on a draft feature film screened in your lounge room. That's really valuable." —Perri Cummings, producer *Trench*

If it's not possible to do an in-person group screening, ask fans to watch the full-film draft from the comfort of their own home. Send a link to the video, with an expiry date, and follow up with a survey or reaction interview.

The reaction interview is still a crucial tool in this step.

Now there's a full-film draft to show people, it's possible to ask even more specific questions like:
- How would you describe this film without giving away the story or plot twists?
- What would people be saying about this film on their way out of the cinema?
- What would make you want to see this film again?

During interviews remember to listen and learn, not waste time defending what you've made. Because it's lo-fi, you already know there's heaps of work still to be done. You need to become an expert at reading between the lines of what people say about the story, and park comments about the production values for now.

After screenings and interviews, organize the fan feedback in a central place for easy reference.

No decisions need to be made about the feedback right now – that happens in the Adjust stage – but it's good for the whole squad to read all of the feedback provided by fans in preparation.

Adjust

The third stage in the cycle is Adjust. It includes analyzing the fan feedback, determining the outcome of the tests, organizing fan experience improvements and reflecting on the workflow.

There are also two major ceremonies in the Adjust stage: the fan experience improvement review and squad retrospective.

The fan experience improvement review happens at the start of the Adjust stage.

During this review, the squad discusses improvements, using the Story Scaffold to ground the discussion and as a reference for the current version of the film. The squad decides which improvements succeeded or failed, based on feedback gathered in the cycle.

Write new or adjusted improvements on index cards (and trash those that aren't relevant anymore).

Remember each fan experience improvement is written in this standard format: Improve the film by [insert fan experience improvement] so fans feel [insert emotion].

Assigning a size, like small/medium/large, to each improvement helps estimate how many can be implemented in a cycle.

This ceremony isn't for deciding how to execute these improvements – that happens in cycle planning.

In this review, the squad ranks the improvements in order from the highest priority to the lowest on the Story Scaffold backlog.

To maintain the relevancy of the improvements, include backlog grooming in this ceremony.

If improvements have been lingering in the backlog for several cycles, they may be too large, poorly articulated or not worth the effort anymore. Feel free to discard any improvements that no longer serve the film.

At the end of this ceremony, the fan experience is revisited to ensure it still accurately reflects the goals of the film.

A few words of caution.

It's tempting to debate improvements (and the story in general) for a *really* long time.

It feels productive.

It feels like you're getting somewhere.

It feels safer to talk about the film, rather than make and show fans the film in progress.

But all improvements are abstract until they're tested and validated. The squad is encouraged to favor evidence over opinion or gut feelings.

Avoid becoming mired in prolonged talk-fests by setting a strict time limit for this ceremony (and indeed for all ceremonies).

There are no perfect decisions that magically solve all story problems – just the best ones made with the information available that propel the squad into action.

Finally, a squad retrospective is held at the end of the Adjust stage to reflect on the workflow and make refinements for the next cycle.

There are many different ways to run retrospectives. This is our favorite place to start.

Draw a symbol on sticky notes to represent each category of reflection and put them up on a wall:
☺ What worked?
☹ What didn't work?
😕 What was confusing?

Set a timer for three minutes. Everyone silently writes sticky notes with their ideas about these categories.

Each person then takes turns putting their sticky notes up on the wall under the appropriate category, briefly describing each one without interruption from the other squad members. Any similar ideas can be grouped together.

When all the sticky notes are up, the squad discusses the ideas as a group to acknowledge progress, resolve any obvious miscommunications and decide what can be done better.

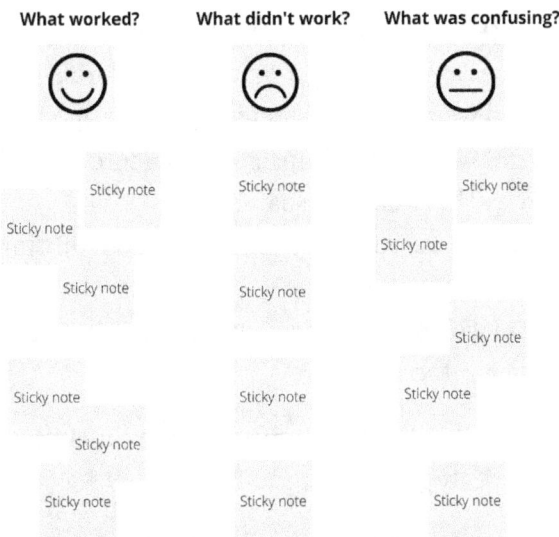

The squad can also use dot voting to agree on workflow processes to address in the next cycle. Each person votes by using a marker to draw a dot on the ideas they think are the highest priority. Everyone gets three dots and they can be used all on one idea or spread across several ideas. The idea(s) with the most dots is executed in the next cycle.

For example, things that the squad may want to address include:
- × Are we communicating in a way that's suitable for everyone?
- × Are everyone's skills being utilized in the best way?
- × Are we attempting too many fan experience improvements in the cycle?

- Is this the best rehearsal process for our actors?
- Does anyone need additional help during the shoot?
- Did we waste time focusing on just one stage?
- Did we document insights from interviews in a way that's easy to share?
- Did we recruit enough fans, at the right time, to fill a screening?
- Do we need a new screening venue as the current one is too small?

Remember, this ceremony specifically addresses how the squad works together, not the story.

As mentioned in Step 1, even though squads are cross-functional, it doesn't mean that roles don't exist. It's up to the squad to decide who does which role(s) and how tasks are allocated, creating new opportunities for the work to be done in different ways.

The squad retrospective provides a structure to detect and resolve problems as they emerge, rather than letting them fester and blow up.

It's important to reiterate how crucial psychological safety is for successfully running this ceremony.

Everyone has permission to express themselves candidly in an environment of mutual respect, without fear of repercussions or negative consequences. Anyone on the squad can raise questions about ethics, equity, representation and responsibilities.

This allows for compassionate, honest and thoughtful conversations about inevitable failures, weaknesses and fuck-ups.

Repeat

Then do it all again. Keep repeating the cycle of Make-Show-Adjust until the squad has achieved Story–Fan Fit.

Embrace the concept of test and learn. Enjoy the freedom to make mistakes, discover the unexpected and excavate the truth of a story.

Our biggest piece of advice: don't be too precious during the full-film draft cycles!

In our hypothetical example for *Solo Woman Traveler*, the squad did four full-film drafts in standard MSA Cycles. Our cadence was one cycle every four weeks.

Obviously zombie films rely heavily on special effects, makeup and costumes – but before investing in any of that, we wanted a killer story.

These were the main improvements in each MSA Cycle:

Draft 1
Used stock footage, storyboards and simple scenes with our two actors to get the basics of the idea.

Draft 2
Focused on developing the main character, key relationships and central conflicts. We discovered our

fans liked the idea that office workers were zombies who wanted the free-spirited backpackers to assimilate.

Draft 3

Added specific nuances about backpacking, including the skills gained while solo traveling to help slay zombies, one-liners and in-jokes. We concentrated on giving every zombie movie trope a hostel twist but fans thought that was too on-the-nose so they were trashed.

Draft 4

Increased dramatic tension, added more character beats into the action sequences, raised the stakes and developed our zombie mythology.

Our squad partnered with a local hostel for free use of their recreation room, giving us a monthly screening time as a firm deadline for showing fans the drafts. This also helped us understand how the film played in its intended environment, plus a space for reaction interviews and access to new potential fans. During this step we grew our email list to more than two hundred fans.

We tested if *Solo Woman Traveler* also appealed to general fans of the undead action-comedy genre during the release of a big Hollywood zombie movie. We politely ambushed people after screenings of the film on opening weekend, showing them our most recent trailer and asking for feedback. While overall it got a positive response, we struggled to discern a clear way to reach these fans.

This reassured us that the right move was to continue focusing on our core backpacking cohorts of fans.

You're done with this step when...

You've got a full-film draft that's achieved Story–Fan Fit.

You've validated the story with fan feedback from screenings, retrospectives, interviews and surveys and the full-film draft predictably elicits the intended fan experience.

You've grown your email list and created basic marketing materials that consistently engage new fans.

As a squad, you're proficient at running standard MSA Cycles, including all ceremonies.

You might also be done if the squad *hasn't* found Story–Fan Fit but has run out of time, money or energy.

In this case, the squad has got a choice to make:
- × Do Step 2 again but pivot to a new cohort of fans
- × Do Step 2 again but pivot to a new idea for a different film
- × Quit (or take a long break)

And we really want you to hear this – quitting isn't a bad option!

There's zero shame in calling it quits, especially if you're sacrificing your mental health, emptying your bank balance and eroding relationships with family and friends. Filmmaking shouldn't be do or die.

Creating an independent feature film, regardless of the method, is a hard slog – but an advantage of Lean Filmmaking is being able to responsibly abandon a project if it has little chance of success, before investing too much.

But if the squad has achieved Story–Fan Fit, they'll need to determine resourcing, especially as production values will be added in the next step. Finally!

Creative problem-solving and inventiveness still win over splashing cash. Improvements that add production values still need to be tested in a methodical way with MSA Cycles.

Through fan feedback and research, the squad should have an understanding about the size of the potential market, allowing them to make smart decisions about the level of investment.

Lastly, hold another Go/No Go Meeting to confirm the commitment of all squad members and decide the work schedule. The squad may benefit from some more intensive periods of time to complete full-film drafts.

If you can complete the below checklist, and understand the tools, you're ready to move on to the next step.

Step 3 Checklist
- Construct initial Story Scaffold
- Develop full-film drafts in standard MSA Cycles (including ceremonies)
- Increase fan email list
- Test basic marketing materials
- Set date for next Go/No Go Meeting
- Commit to schedule and budget for the next step

Step 3 Tools
- Story Scaffold
- Fan experience improvements
- Standard Make-Show-Adjust Cycles (including ceremonies)
- Fan screening: free
- Fan review

Step 4: Produce Polishes

It's pivotal to find the connection between a well-crafted film and the fans who want to buy it.

The fourth step in the Lean Filmmaking method is to produce full-film polishes until it's proven that fans will purchase and recommend the film.

As well as the benefits of learning by doing, there are other advantages to producing polishes, including:
- × Using fan experience improvements to validate production values
- × Incrementally adding production values to reduce financial risk
- × Testing fan intention versus action with paid screenings
- × Avoiding the sunk cost fallacy

You've spent time ensuring your story connects with fans in a lo-fi draft, but in this step you'll focus on crafting the aesthetics that your fans value by producing full-film polishes.

The Lean Filmmaking Method

Step 1: Form Squad

Validate: Squad goals

↓

Step 2: Discover Fans

Validate: Fan experience
 ✘ Tester videos
 ✘ Reaction interviews

↓

Step 3: Develop Drafts

Validate: Story–Fan Fit
 ✘ Full-film drafts
 ✘ Free fan screenings
 ✘ Story improvements

↓

Step 4: Produce Polishes

Validate: Production–Fan Fit
 ✘ **Full-film polishes**
 ✘ **Paid fan screenings**
 ✘ **Production improvements**

↓

Step 5: Launch Film

Validate: Distribution strategy

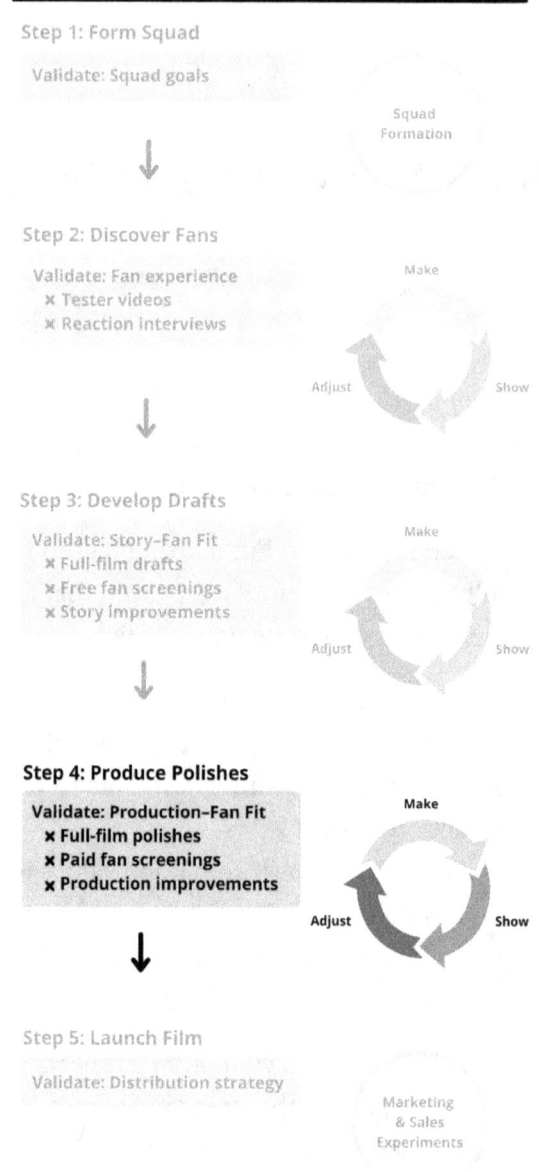

Full-film Polishes

Hi-fi versions of the entire film made in Make-Show-Adjust Cycles, using technical craft skills to apply appropriate production values that deliver the fan experience, ultimately finding Production-Fan Fit.

The squad uses their creativity to improve the aesthetics, adding sound design, special effects, costumes, locations, music, background actors and all of the other things that round out a well-crafted film.

Yay! Bring on the glossy production values!

But at the risk of sounding like the fun police, don't go wild just yet.

Every change still needs to be tested with fans to give the film the greatest chance of success. Only incorporate elements that fans consider important; don't over-invest in expensive improvements that fans couldn't care less about.

There'll be a strong temptation to do a big final cycle to get everything perfect "once and for all".

Please, please, please, resist this urge.

It's a seductive fantasy to believe all of the film's issues can be solved in one cycle.

But there's a real risk that a large one-and-done cycle could kill your project.

It's heartbreaking to waste time, money and energy on a production-values-packed cycle that fails to deliver the fan experience as anticipated.

Hi-fi changes are often expensive to execute and can easily blow the budget, making it tough for an independent film to recoup the costs if they don't work. It's better to mitigate the financial risk by incrementally rolling out smaller changes in cycles.

During this step it's also common to fall prey to the sunk cost fallacy.

A sunk cost has already been paid and can't be recovered. The sunk cost fallacy is our desire to keep following a plan if we've already invested time, effort and money.

It's a powerful fallacy to be aware of because we assume people make rational decisions about investments, but this isn't always the case. Even though sunk costs should be irrelevant to future decisions, the more we invest in a plan of action, the stronger our emotional attachment and the more reluctant we are to abandon it.

This kind of thinking is rampant in traditional filmmaking due to the linear nature of the process.

For example, it's common practice to overshoot during production. As part of standard coverage, it's normal to shoot multiple takes of the same scene from different angles to ensure there'll be plenty of choices during editing in post-production. Most of this footage is never used and ends up on the cutting room floor.

Not only is this an incredibly wasteful process, but there's another unintended consequence.

Filmmakers get attached to the footage because they know how much effort was involved to get it.

They worked long days, sometimes in brutally harsh conditions, to get beautiful shots. It's tough to let them go – even if they no longer serve the film and actually hurt its financial and critical success.

Traditional filmmaking expects projects will go over budget and be delayed. It's easier to continue down a planned course of action. Even when conditions change or new information comes to light, it's often ignored because of excessive optimism, unwillingness to admit failure and an aversion to the loss of the sunk costs.

In Lean Filmmaking, we don't want you to throw good money after bad.

Gradually adding production values in cycles helps the squad make pragmatic decisions, accept failure as part of the learning process and avoid the painful consequences of the sunk cost fallacy.

Before moving onto the mechanics of producing full-film polishes, let's discuss the purpose of paid fan screenings and how to scale the squad and prioritize production values.

Ask fans to pay for it

One of the new challenges in this step is asking fans to pay to view the film.

We finalize the distribution strategy in the next step, but right now you'll have to come to grips with asking fans to open their wallets.

By now you're a pro at asking for feedback – remember how uncomfortable that made you in the beginning?

You'll also get more comfortable asking for sales.

But we're not going to lie.

The first time you ask someone to pay for an unfinished film is probably going to be pretty painful.

As filmmakers, we're not encouraged to show our work until it's perfect. You've made great strides by showing your full-film drafts to fans for free, but you're likely to have some resistance to charging a fee for an imperfect version of the film.

While it's great if people like, comment and share, there's another level of important support: spending money. People can easily *say* they'll buy your film – sometimes if only to get out of an awkward conversation – but when they pull out their credit card, things get real.

The reason squads need to do paid screenings is to test intention versus action.

It's essential the squad knows what will make people pay for their film (and not just say they might buy it down the track). And to test this, real money must be on the line.

Of course, because it's not the finished film, it's okay to ask for a token amount.

You're not trying to make money, yet. You're testing the market.

And it's easy to give refunds. If a fan wants a refund, politely return their money and apologize without any defensiveness. (Ideally, do a reaction interview with them!)

Refunds also provide vital information. If a few people want refunds, that can be accounted for by personal taste, but if numerous fans ask for their money back, or stop participating in any feedback after initially being enthusiastic, something deeper may need to be addressed.

Positive feedback feels good but there's far more to learn from harsh criticism.

It's better to know now so you can make improvements, rather than when the film is completed.

Running screenings requires the squad to consistently recruit fans.

We've included this work in the Show stage of MSA Cycles, but in reality, finding fans is ongoing and can happen at any time. To reduce unwanted delays, organizing the screening and selling tickets during the Make stage will ensure that the Show stage runs smoothly.

"We ended up with a film that we knew had fans, and were confident we could reach them when it was released." —Melanie Rowland, producer *Time Apart*

If the squad validates that a large percentage of their fans are willing to purchase, they can confidently invest more money to polish the film.

Scale the squad (but only if you really need to)

To deliver full-film polishes, additional talent may be needed to complement the squad's skillset.

An obvious example, with the most immediate impact, are supporting actors to play characters that will enhance the subplots.

The level of participation of supporting actors can be decided by the squad. The new actors could take part in MSA Cycles including ceremonies, or they may just film their scenes in short bursts, during the Make stage. The squad can trial different ways of working in cycles.

Some other ways to scale the squad may include finding a composer to write a score, a colorist to do a color grade or an audio engineer for a sound mix.

By now, the squad knows if there are any gaps in their skills and what value other people can offer.

But you don't have to bring more people onto the squad if you don't want to.

The squad may decide the disadvantages of more people outweigh the benefits. By keeping the number of people working on the film to a minimum, there's no need to worry about the higher degree of complexity or building trust with new squad members.

Any change to the squad, even positive, will affect team dynamics.

And it's easy to let traditional practices creep in, especially if there isn't a fundamental understanding of Lean Filmmaking philosophy.

As discussed in Step 1, maximizing collaboration requires two big paradigm shifts:
- × The director doesn't have authority to give unilateral commands
- × The cast and crew have autonomy and take responsibility for their area of expertise

This is a radical change for most people. If the squad scales, make space for extra training, allow additional time to run ceremonies and expect some growing pains.

The squad should consider how to manage payments, ownership and copyright. They could use deferred fee agreements or might be in the financial position to pay work-for-hire contracts. There'll also be implications for health and safety plans, permits and insurance.

Prioritize with the Impact-vs-Difficulty Matrix

It's challenging to decide which production values – and the associated fan experience improvements – to work on first, because these choices often require a trade-off between quality and cost.

To help make informed decisions, the squad can use an Impact-vs-Difficulty Matrix as a way to prioritize fan experience improvements.

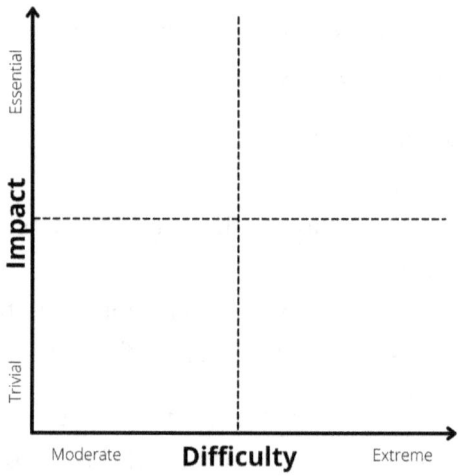

One axis of the matrix represents the level of impact from trivial to essential, and the other axis is the degree of difficulty from moderate to extreme, making four quadrants.

The degree of impact can be assessed by the feedback fans have repeatedly given about an area of concern. Production values that are nice-to-have but not crucial to improving the fan experience must be deemed low impact.

For example, if fans constantly provide strong feedback that the fast-moving camerawork distracts them from the story, this will have a higher degree of impact, rather than a small technical detail that no-one has ever mentioned.

The degree of difficulty can be assessed by the squad, using measures like the number of scenes affected, extra costs, additional actors or the amount of time it would take to execute.

For example, setting the film in a different time period might be difficult as it requires substantial changes to every scene, but a few flashbacks could be incorporated without major disruption. Or a specific location that's expensive, inconvenient and only open at night will have a higher degree of difficulty than shooting in an easily accessible place that's available any time.

If an improvement has a high degree of difficulty, it might be the only one to be focused on in a cycle. If there are several easier, high-impact improvements, they could be done together in one cycle.

Just because something is difficult, doesn't mean that it shouldn't be done – as long as it's also high impact.

But it's in the squad's best interest to completely avoid the changes that are low impact and high difficulty, or at the very least, postpone until later cycles.

The squad can use the matrix during the fan experience improvement review to provide a structure for evaluating risks and rewards.

Draw the matrix on a whiteboard or delineate quadrants with sticky notes on a wall.

Set a timer for three minutes. Everyone silently writes sticky notes with production values ideas – these can come from the Story Scaffold backlog or be totally new.

Each person then takes turns plotting their sticky notes on the matrix based on their perceived level of impact and degree of difficulty, briefly describing each one without interruption from the other squad members. Group any similar ideas together.

When all the sticky notes are plotted on the matrix, the squad discusses the ideas as a group and decides which ideas warrant testing. They are then written as fan experience improvements and prioritized on the Story Scaffold backlog, ready for the next cycle.

Run full-film polish Make-Show-Adjust Cycles

It's time to take the lessons learned from developing drafts and apply them to producing full-film polishes.

Full-film polishes are completed in an iterative way using standard MSA Cycles in a predetermined cadence. All squad members are involved in every stage.

The squad evaluates ways to improve the fan experience through gradually increasing production values, with a goal of achieving Production–Fan Fit.

Production–Fan Fit
A strong connection between a well-crafted film and the fans who want to purchase it. This is achieved by using Make-Show-Adjust Cycles to produce full-film polishes that validate production values with fans.

As the cycles continue, the squad validates technical improvements but can also test the size of their potential market and how much (or if at all) fans are willing to pay for the film.

As discussed in Part 1, the work of planning, filming and learning is organized into small continuous cycles. The squads make, show and adjust tester videos (Step 2), then full-film drafts (Step 3) and full-film polishes (Step 4), before converging on the final version of the film.

The key actions in each standard MSA Cycle for full-film polishes are the same as the previous step:

Make
- × Cycle planning
- × Make full-film polish
- × Standups

Show
- Recruit fans
- Show full-film polish
- Collect fan feedback

Adjust
- Analyze fan feedback
- Fan experience improvement review
- Squad retrospective

Make

Once again, the first stage in the cycle is Make. It includes all of the work required to complete a full-film polish like writing, acting, shooting, directing and editing. It has the same ceremonies as draft cycles, but the focus is on polishing the film by adding production values.

During the cycle planning, the squad commits to the amount of work as an achievable goal for the cycle. The squad choses the appropriate number of fan experience improvements from the Story Scaffold backlog and the tests to be conducted. These are broken down into discrete tasks to be completed in the cycle.

Then the squad makes the full-film polish, using standups to ensure the work is on track and the squad is communicating any issues to be resolved.

Show

The second stage in the cycle is Show. It includes showing the full-film polish and collecting feedback from fans. This is the time to recruit more fans (if the squad hasn't already done so in the Make stage).

As the film becomes more polished, the marketing materials can also be refined. The squad can revise their trailer, poster and synopsis, and test film titles in preparation for the final version.

The email list is still a crucial marketing tool. Building a simple one-page website with an opt-in to collect email addresses is an easy way to ensure that it keeps growing.

It may also be useful to start a basic online community for fans, like a Facebook group, Mighty Network or subreddit, as a place to experiment with marketing materials and sell screening tickets.

Even though it's tempting, don't put any effort into branding yet, unless you already have an established presence. It's time-consuming and wasted effort until you're sure about the platforms your fans are active on. (In the next step we discuss running experiments to validate marketing and sales strategies.)

The squad shows the full-film polish to paying fans, either with an in-person screening or online, and collects feedback. The squad can use all of the methods of feedback from the previous two steps including surveys, reaction interviews and fan retrospectives.

The goal is to see if improvements made in the cycle have succeeded – or failed – to positively impact the fan experience and test the market viability of the film.

Run a paid in-person fan screening
Paid fan screenings require a higher degree of coordination and professionalism that comes with charging a fee.

First of all, the squad needs a simple way to take bookings and collect money.

It can be lo-fi, like a simple RSVP list and people pay cash at the door. Or a little more hi-fi, like an online ticketing system to process payments and scan entry with a smartphone app.

Because this isn't the final film, the squad can test different ticket prices – just make sure to cover any costs of hosting the screening.

Then the squad has to find a venue, preferably a free or low-cost alternative to cinemas, at least for the first few cycles.

For example, some bars, pubs or hotels have screening rooms that are free with a minimum spend on drinks. Co-working offices often have event spaces for hire, or sometimes at no charge with in-kind sponsorship. If the film's theme speaks directly to a specialty group that holds regular meetings, the organizers could be interested in hosting a screening for their members.

After multiple cycles, and when the squad is confident they're in the final stages of testing, it may be worthwhile to hire a cinema – but figure out how many tickets must be sold to cover costs and plan accordingly.

Once the venue is secured, start selling tickets. Manage expectations by including information that the film is a work in progress and feedback will be important.

Ideally, you'll have at least twenty people attend the screening. Scan tickets, tick off an RSVP list or count attendees, to record the number of attendees and no-shows for later reference.

Before showing the film, it's a great idea to do a welcome speech and introduce the squad. Remind attendees that it's a work in progress, ask them for their feedback after the screening and thank them for their support.

You'll very badly want to say that the film is really rough, the budget was small and there are so many things that still need to be finished.

Don't. Do. This.

Keep disclaimers to a minimum.

The goal is to get people's honest reaction to the film and not preempt their experience. The same rules about priming, from research interviews in Step 2, applies here.

Then show the film.

It's ideal for all squad members to attend these screenings and take notes. Watching the film with an audience is enlightening: do the jokes hit; are people laughing, crying, gasping in the right places; how is the atmosphere in the room; are people engaged or wriggling in their seats?

After screening the full-film polish, get feedback.

It's ideal for the squad to facilitate a fan review. Depending on the number of attendees, be prepared to split into smaller groups. (Instructions for running a fan review are in Step 3.)

If attendees don't want to take part in group feedback, have a survey prepared to be filled out before the fans leave the screening, including opt-in permission for the email list, suggested referrals and request for a reaction interview (to be done online or in person).

After the attendees leave, the squad can make notes about the feedback gathered during the fan review in preparation for the fan experience improvement review.

Run a paid online fan screening
Follow the same process as running an in-person screening but instead of finding a venue, the squad will use an online streaming or video on demand platform to host the screening.

The squad can either run an online screening at a set time for a group of fans or allow fans to watch it alone in their own time.

Tickets can be purchased the same way as an in-person event, but the price may be lower. Once a purchase is made, send an email with the screening link and password, depending on the platform.

If it's a live screening with multiple fans, there may be a group chat as everyone experiences it together.

If fans are watching it by themselves, make sure to include an expiry date and get their feedback in a timely way.

After the screening, follow up with an online survey or reaction interview. Fan reviews are easier to do in person but can also be conducted online with a video conference call – it just requires more coordination.

Compile the feedback results ready for the fan experience improvement review.

Adjust

The third stage in the cycle is Adjust. It includes analyzing the fan feedback, determining the outcome of the tests, organizing fan experience improvements and reflecting on the workflow.

During the fan experience improvement review, use the Impact-vs-Difficulty Matrix to prioritize improvements for the next cycle that focus on adding production values.

At the end of this ceremony, the squad briefly revisits the fan experience, but there shouldn't be any dramatic pivots at this stage.

During the squad retrospective, make adjustments to the process and resolve any issues that surfaced during the cycle, especially if the squad has scaled to include new members.

Repeat

Then do it all again.

Keep repeating the cycle of Make-Show-Adjust until the squad has achieved Production–Fan Fit. The film consistently delivers the fan experience and can't be improved any more within the limitations of their constraints.

Cycles are done. The final version of the film is done.

You're amazing. Congratulations!

One final thing (and this is really important).

The film will never be perfect.

But it is the very best film the squad can make given their resources, skills, talents and creativity.

In our hypothetical example for *Solo Woman Traveler*, the squad completed three full-film polishes in standard MSA Cycles. Our cadence was one cycle every five weeks.

In the first cycle, almost all of the material was new. As we got closer to completion, there were fewer large-scale changes that impacted the entire film. Only 10% was new in the last cycle, but those few additional production values were important final flourishes.

These were the main improvements in the MSA Cycles:

Polish 1
Added practical in-camera effects, experimented with basic special effects makeup and added background actors to key scenes. (90% of the full film was new in this version.)

Polish 2
Scaled the squad to include a stunt coordinator, a specialist makeup artist and two supporting actors, all on deferred fees. Concentrated on shooting in every different area of the hostel to maximize the unique location. (40% of the full film was new in this version.)

Polish 3
Filmed a large set piece (super fun party scene with a hundred background actors) and hired a freelance visual effects editor and sound engineer. (10% of the full film was new in this version.)

We embraced our constraints and set the film in one practical location – a backpackers hostel. We secured free location hire from our hostel partner, provided we filmed during off-peak times and purchased catering from their on-site cafe (at a reasonable rate).

To save costs, we used backpackers staying in the hostel as background actors, paying them with pizza and beer. They got a free meal and a fun experience; we got a ready reserve of background actors.

But our fans demanded at least some special effects, fight sequences, makeup and costumes to deliver on the zombie genre.

Prior to this step, we'd only spent a nominal amount of money, but we now needed to invest some funds to complete the film. The four original squad members each personally invested $2,500, to be recouped first from any film sales. We also held a fundraising event for family, friends and fans that raised another $2,000, for a total production budget of $12,000.

We used this to pay for professional zombie makeup materials (including lots of fake blood), specialist gear for stunts, extra props and costumes. And of course, catering.

We paid a freelance visual effects editor to enhance several sequences and hired a sound engineer with their own studio for the final audio mix.

We invited everyone on our email list, which we'd grown to seven hundred fans, to be in the film as party guests for a large set piece. At the end of the shoot, we had a real party to thank everyone for their support.

It took our squad twelve months to go from idea to final film, working on a consistent part-time basis around day jobs. By traditional film industry standards, this is an extraordinarily fast turnaround!

You're done with this step when...

You've got a full-film polish that's achieved Production–Fan Fit.

You've validated the production values with fan feedback from screenings, retrospectives, interviews and surveys, and the full-film polish predictably elicits the intended fan experience.

You've got an engaged community of fans willing to pay for the film and actively recommend it to other people.

You've got polished marketing materials that consistently convert new fans to attend paid screenings, sign up to the email list and join the community.

As a squad, you've determined that adding more production values won't substantially increase the satisfaction of the fan experience for the majority of your fans.

You might also be done if the squad *hasn't* found Production–Fan fit but has run out of time, money or energy.

In this case, the squad has got a choice to make:
- × Do Step 2 again but pivot to a new cohort of fans
- × Do Step 2 again but pivot to a new idea for a different film
- × Quit (or take a long break)

Even now after all of this hard work, quitting is still not a bad option!

Remember the sunk cost fallacy.

The squad can take everything they've learned on this project and apply it to a new idea, rather than persist with a film they haven't been able to sell, despite their best efforts.

But if the squad has achieved Production–Fan Fit, the end is in sight.

In the last step, the squad leverages everything they've learned from fans to distribute the film.

There'll be some film delivery costs, but as the squad knows the size of their market, these expenses can be in proportion to realistic sales income.

Do one more Go/No Go Meeting and confirm the agreement from all squad members about their commitment for the final step.

If you can complete the below checklist, and understand the tools, you're ready to move on to the next step.

Step 4 Checklist
- Scale squad (if required)
- Produce full-film polishes in standard MSA Cycles (including ceremonies)
- Grow fan email list
- Start fan community
- Polish marketing materials
- Set date for next Go/No Go Meeting
- Commit to schedule and budget for the next step

Step 4 Tools
- Impact-vs-Difficulty Matrix
- Fan screening: paid

Step 5: Launch Film

To launch a film, it's important to communicate the fan experience in a compelling way, and find distribution channels and marketing strategies that consistently make sales.

The fifth step in the Lean Filmmaking method is running sales and marketing experiments that successfully launch the film to fans.

Most independent filmmakers face a stark realization when they finish a feature film: the work is far from done. They've still got to distribute it!

It's tempting to think good films will reach fans based on their merit, but that's rarely the case.

Ultimately it's the squad's responsibility to sell, market and launch their film.

Luckily, you're already way ahead of the game.

The Lean Filmmaking Method

Step 1: Form Squad

    Validate: Squad goals

Step 2: Discover Fans

    Validate: Fan experience
        ✘ Tester videos
        ✘ Reaction interviews

Step 3: Develop Drafts

    Validate: Story-Fan Fit
        ✘ Full-film drafts
        ✘ Free fan screenings
        ✘ Story improvements

Step 4: Produce Polishes

    Validate: Production-Fan Fit
        ✘ Full-film polishes
        ✘ Paid fan screenings
        ✘ Production improvements

Step 5: Launch Film

Validate: Distribution strategy

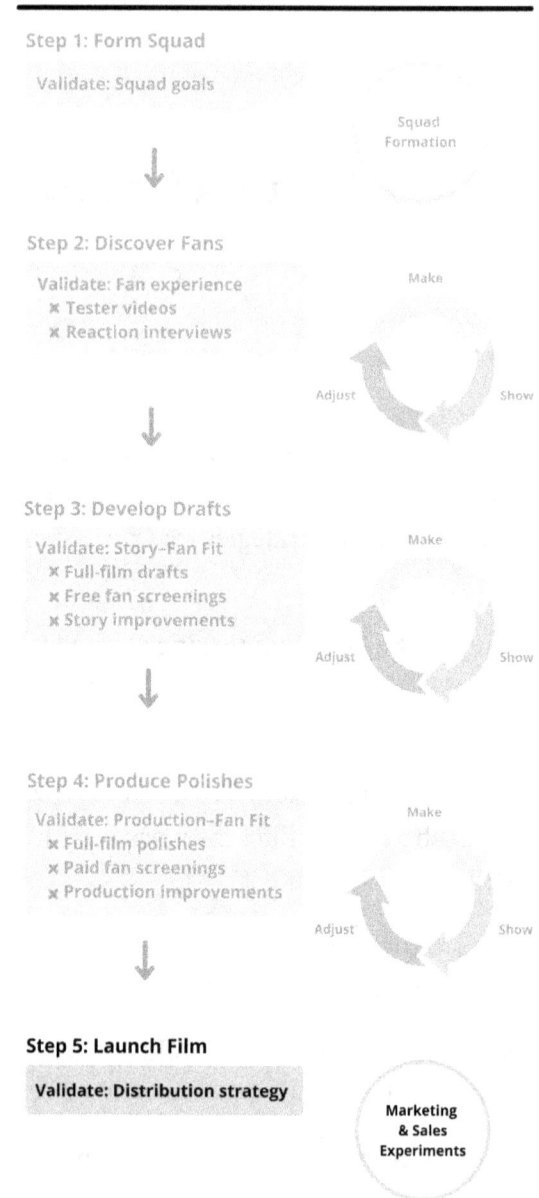

You've tested marketing materials and sold film screenings.

You know who your fans are and how to reach them.

You've decided what accomplishment looks like for *your* squad, even if it's not what the film industry would normally use as a measure of success.

The squad's goals inform how the film will be launched and sold.

Even if the squad has non-financial goals, like raising awareness of an issue, increasing their credibility as artists or building a strong community for future projects, they'll still need a distribution strategy to reach fans.

Now is a good time to reiterate: there isn't an expectation to have reached *all* of your fans in the previous steps. You just needed enough fans to validate your film. There'll be fans that have been with you since the beginning and followed the whole journey, but they're only a small sample of your total audience.

Really, only dedicated fans, cinephiles and other filmmakers are interested in the nitty-gritty of movie production.

Most people only care about watching a well-crafted film that's tailored to their interests.

The majority of fans will enjoy the final film, never having been involved in the early drafting or polishing stages, and without ever knowing anything about Lean Filmmaking.

In this step, the squad expands their initial fanbase to convert new fans in a repeatable sales pipeline.

"With its focus on fans, it's an incredibly smart way to get filmmakers to not only think about the end pipeline from the start, but to find, cultivate and maintain the kind of audience that connects with exactly what they're out to communicate." —Perri Cummings, producer *Trench*

"Filmmakers rarely get taught the importance of audience development and marketing – which for an independent filmmaker looking to make a living on their craft, is actually vital." —Melanie Rowland, producer *Time Apart*

One more caveat.

Just like this book works best for those who already have an understanding of filmmaking fundamentals, the same applies for the basics of marketing. Marketing is a large subject and impossible for us to cover in depth.

It's highly advantageous to have a skilled marketing person in the squad or access to a marketing professional to consult on the film. There are also many great resources available online to learn more about marketing.

Instead, we'll focus on the opportunities of self-distribution and running sales and marketing experiments to maximize the launch of the film.

But before we move on, we need to have a tough-love conversation about film festivals.

Stop obsessing about film festivals

Many independent filmmakers have the same dream for their debut feature film: a world premiere at a prestigious festival like Sundance, Cannes, Toronto, Venice or Berlin.

Acceptance into a top-tier festival, standing ovations and a hotly contested sale for a shit-ton of money are seen as the benchmark of critical success for indie films.

But this happens a lot less than you think.

Let's be clear: we love film festivals.

They have a very special place in our hearts.

Kylie has spent more than a decade working for arts and film festivals, traveled to international festivals with her feature film and regularly speaks and facilitates workshops at festivals.

Festivals bring together filmmakers from all walks of life, providing a sense of belonging and community.

Seeing your film up on the big screen and sharing it with an audience is a powerful moment. It's a celebration that makes all the blood, sweat and tears seem worthwhile.

Attending film festivals has other drawcards, like networking with peers, being creatively inspired, gaining industry knowledge and going to parties (let's face it, the parties are great).

And even if you don't attend the festival, the film can still garner prestige, industry recognition, positive reviews and maybe even win an award. At the very least, you'll have a festival laurel for your marketing materials.

It all sounds fantastic, right?

Well, first you have to get into a festival.

High-profile festivals get *thousands* of entries every year. For a real chance at being selected, films need a local distributor, sales agent, track record or A-list actor.

Without these elements, acceptance into a festival isn't impossible – but it's more akin to winning the lottery than a reliable distribution strategy.

And rejection from a festival isn't necessarily a reflection of a film's worthiness or value.

Not only is the selection process competitive, but programmers have to consider other factors – many outside the filmmaker's control – like country of origin, premiere status, genre, style and themes.

There's also an unpredictable spark, call it good timing or the zeitgeist, that can magically turn a film into a festival darling (when in any other year it could've been overlooked).

There are two more downsides that make film festival distribution risky: the cost of delay and low chance of attracting new fans.

Submitting to festivals is a time killer. Prestigious festivals want world premiere status. It's the first time your film is screened publicly – obviously you only get one shot at this.

Months can be wasted waiting to be rejected from your first preference before moving down the list to other festivals. Depending on your film's completion date and festival deadlines, it can literally take years to make the rounds of the festival circuit – valuable time that's better spent selling your film to a paying audience before the film becomes irrelevant.

After spending a substantial amount of money, energy and time, if you *do* get into a festival, there's still no guarantee it will translate into more fans for your film.

Festivals have different objectives than filmmakers – it's their job to build their own audience, not one for your film. All your work understanding fans doesn't matter in these circumstances and probably won't align with the festival's marketing.

Festivals often screen hundreds of films. Their focus is on marketing the whole program, rather than individual titles, unless the film has A-list actors or a recognized auteur director.

It's easy for a film to get lost in the pack, especially if it only has one screening in a crappy timeslot. But even if a film has multiple sessions, and sells out, it won't be seen by many people. Maybe a thousand, probably a lot less.

These audiences are often seen as tastemakers, and positive word-of-mouth may bring extra attention, but it might not be enough to warrant the effort.

Of course, there are exceptions.

If a film caters to a well-defined niche (like LGBTQIA+, environment/sustainability or human rights) or genre (like horror or sci-fi) and can target specialty festivals that serve these audiences, it'll have a better chance of selection and finding die-hard fans.

But if you really want to build your own community, festivals aren't going to cut it.

If the squad decides to pursue a festival release strategy, increase the odds of selection by doing research.

Read interviews with the programmers, talk to filmmakers who've screened at the festival and interrogate the kind of films that have been accepted in the past. Spend time on FilmFreeway researching the number of festivals in your niche or genre plus screening fees, entry requirements and deadlines, to determine if it's a viable option.

All of this isn't to crush your film festival dreams.

We want you to carefully consider the advantages, and disadvantages, of festivals when deciding how to sell your film.

Awards, accolades and festival laurels – while very nice – pale in comparison to passionate fans and a profitable film.

Being able to keep making feature films because you've found a way to create a sustainable business is a great reward too.

We've challenged you to look at film production through a new lens, and now we're doing the same with distribution.

Demystify self-distribution

Distribution is often a daunting, confusing and convoluted process that can feel very overwhelming.

In the past, gatekeepers like studios, distributors and exhibitors had all the power to dictate which films audiences would see. And they've had a notorious reputation for silencing marginalized voices, discouraging diversity and lacking inclusivity.

But self-distribution is your new best friend. There's an ever-increasing variety of distribution channels that are accessible to everyone.

You don't need permission from the gatekeepers to make your film anymore.

Your unique voice can be heard.

You're in the perfect position to find radical new ways to self-distribute your film.

Self-distribution

Selling a film directly to fans, rather than selling it to a distributor. The film's producers get their revenue from their customers. It's labor-intensive but there's a capacity to earn a higher percentage of the profits and retain creative control.

In an effort to demystify self-distribution, let's look at some of the opportunities for independent filmmakers.

Theatrical

If the squad decides to take their film to the big screen, there are a few ways to do a theatrical release without a traditional distributor.

Four-walling: hiring a cinema (all "four walls") for a fixed fee and retaining the box office revenue. This service is commonly provided by independent cinemas, rather than mainstream cinema chains, and includes ticketing, logistics and staffing.

While it may be a good option for a one-off screening, it's challenging to manage at scale. It's also expensive and risky. The venue hire is paid upfront, regardless of ticket sales, so it's best used in circumstances when it's clear the screening will cover costs and generate income.

Cinema on Demand (COD): a crowdsourcing model through a platform that has established relationships with cinemas, using low-traffic times to screen films that appeal to niche audiences. COD platforms include FanForce or Demand.Film.

Screenings only proceed if they reach a tipping point of ticket sales, lowering the financial risk for film producers. The COD platform manages ticket sales and film delivery. The box office revenue is split between the cinema, the COD platform and the film producer.

A successful COD strategy requires dedication to audience development. It's an excellent option for touring a film with special events, like Q&As, but takes a substantial time commitment to coordinate and promote.

Non-film Venue Hire: renting a space not traditionally used to host screenings for a fixed fee and retaining ticket sales income.

An unusual venue may have a lower hire fee, but additional equipment, infrastructure and logistics could be required if it's not set up for screenings, increasing the overall cost.

The investment may still be worthwhile if it contributes to the fan experience, generates marketing opportunities and creates positive word-of-mouth. Be creative!

Just some examples of non-film venues include museums, "haunted" mansions, churches, nursing homes, amphitheaters, warehouses, skateparks, circus tents, motor shows, rooftops or bookshops.

Film Festival: a curated event that screens films for a limited time, in-person or online, often with a theme, genre or regional focus.

As we've discussed, most festivals have a competitive selection process. They're high risk and normally don't generate an income. Unless targeting specialty festivals with demonstrated results in a well-defined niche or genre appropriate for your film, we don't recommend festivals as a reliable self-distribution strategy.

Video on demand

The film industry sure does love an acronym. Here are a few terms that are useful when thinking about online distribution.

Video on Demand (VOD): broad category for all platforms where users choose when and what to watch from a collection of videos streamed to personal screens. Originally started with cable, satellite TV and pay-per-view services, but expanded to include video on demand models delivered over the internet.

Over-the-top (OTT): streaming media service that offers film, TV and video content directly to users over the internet, bypassing traditional broadcast, cable or satellite TV services. OTT is a subset of VOD that currently includes SVOD, TVOD, AVOD and PVOD.

Subscription Video on Demand (SVOD): users enter into a subscription agreement, normally a monthly fee, for access to all content available on the platform without limits. Netflix, Disney+ and Amazon Prime Video are examples of SVOD services. There are also many services specializing in independent cinema like Mubi, Fandor and IndieFlix.

Transactional Video on Demand (TVOD): signing up for the service normally isn't required – rather, the user only pays for the specific content they watch, like iTunes or Google Play.

Advertisement Video on Demand (AVOD): the service is free for users in return for being served ads, like YouTube's free service or free-to-air catch-up network TV.

Premium Video on Demand (PVOD): when films are released across online platforms at the same time as cinemas, often called a day-and-date release. The industry standard for major studio films was a ninety-day exclusive theatrical release window but in some territories it's now sixty or forty-five days. The closure of cinemas during the pandemic forced many studio films to be released directly on OTT services, commanding a high price, sometimes on top of a subscription fee.

Just to make it super confusing, some services operate with mixed models and new players are always being launched into the market.

YouTube is a great example of a mixed model, adding monetization options as it matures.

YouTube started as an AVOD (profit sharing with creators), but now it's also a SVOD (monthly fee for exclusive content and removal of ads), TVOD (one-off

Step 5: LAUNCH FILM 199

purchases for movies and TV series) and PVOC (premium content released at the same time as cinemas – or instead of cinemas). YouTube is continuously innovating in an effort to own the creator ecosystem, introducing paid channel memberships and e-commerce stores for fan merchandise.

To get a film released on any of the major OTTs, there'll still be some third-party negotiations with aggregators or smaller distributors who specialize in independent films. The major platforms don't deal with individuals and require an aggregator as an intermediary.

Aggregators don't normally make assessments about the quality of a film and submit films to OTTs for a flat fee or revenue split. They don't market the film; it's still up to the filmmakers to drive sales to earn revenue from the platforms.

There are also smaller distributors specializing in online distribution. They're more likely to have a selection process for quality control, but have more experience in niche content and can assist with film marketing.

Unfortunately there are some predatory companies providing these services, feeding on filmmakers' desperation to get their film distributed. Do your due diligence, get referrals from other filmmakers, seek legal advice before signing contracts and watch out for scams.

If you want to retain the rights to sell on other platforms including your own website, check that your agreements with these companies are non-exclusive.

By knowing the value of your film, and understanding your fans, you don't have to be pressured into a shitty deal.

You can also bypass all of the major players and go full do-it-yourself mode.

Set up your own website and use a back-end service like Vimeo OTT or Gumroad to manage the payments, downloads and streaming. These services normally charge a monthly fee and/or a percentage of each sale. You have access to analytics and customer information to optimize your marketing efforts.

These platforms also allow different pricing levels, so you could offer a premium version of the film that includes bonus materials to add value for your most passionate fans, an educational version for students or a home screening pack.

You've done all the hard work building a loyal following of fans. Instead of sending them to another platform, point them to purchase or rent the film from your website for more profit and control.

Some companies provide white-label OTT platforms, like Uscreen, Shift72 and also Vimeo OTT. If you've got a catalogue of films, it may be worth the investment to have your own fully branded SVOD with all the bells and whistles.

As you can see, there are a *lot* of choices. There may be multiple platforms that serve your squad's goals and fan experience but you can always start small.

Crowdfunding

Crowdfunding is the practice of raising investment for a project with a small amount of money from a large number of people through a third-party company like Kickstarter, Indiegogo or Pozible, or a film-specific platform like Seed&Spark.

Normally filmmakers do crowdfunding at the start of a project to raise the production budget. We don't suggest this for a debut feature (but it may be viable for future projects, when squads have a track record and existing fanbase).

Instead, we recommend crowdfunding to pre-sell the film when it's close to completion. Squads need to factor in the effort required to run a successful campaign but it's a great way to test the appetite of fans, validate marketing messages and get an indication of demand, without a lot of financial risk.

There is some reputational risk if the campaign doesn't succeed, but it's far more manageable than a big splashy launch across multiple platforms that falls flat.

All of the major crowdfunding platforms have excellent resources about running campaigns and best practices for success.

Membership

Filmmakers can use a membership platform like Patreon, Mighty Networks or YouTube channel subscriptions to provide access to the film, and other content, in return for a monthly fee.

This is still an unusual way to self-distribute a film but is definitely worth considering, especially if you already have an established audience.

It works particularly well as a freemium model. This means giving away free content, usually on social media, but also having premium content behind a paywall in a paid membership program, like behind-the-scenes content, ask-me-anything sessions, vlogs, podcasts or forums.

This could be a place to share full-film drafts and get feedback, taking advantage of the materials created in MSA Cycles to provide extra value to your most loyal fans.

This strategy works best with an already engaged community and requires a substantial commitment to posting regular content.

Unconventional film sales

This is a catch-all category for anything else that's considered unorthodox (even by self-distribution standards).

This is when all of the deep fan research pays real dividends.

It's an exciting challenge to find unexpected ways to sell your film that most filmmakers ignore. The more unusual, the less competition from other films, making these a gold mine for a creative squad.

Some ideas include hiring a stall at a specialty conference, collaborating with a supplier who shares the same fans or hosting bespoke events (see more suggestions in non-film venues).

The squad can also consider releasing different edits of the film: maybe there's a ten-hour version for extreme fans, and perhaps it's also divided into twenty-two short episodes or eighty micro-episodes. After the feature version is released behind a paywall, can it be distributed on TikTok, Instagram or YouTube? The power of self-distribution is getting to play by your own rules.

It's a lot of work to create an active community of fans. And if fans want more, the squad can build a dynamic universe that goes way beyond one film.

Alternative revenue streams

Finally, squads may get their income from other sources affiliated with the film, rather than directly selling the film to fans.

For example, the squad may give free access to the film and make money from selling merchandise, soundtracks, toys, NFTs, graphic novels, books, courses or education packages.

Squads can also approach brands to sponsor the project in return for bespoke benefits, like special staff screenings or including the film in a customer loyalty program.

As this long list of sales channels demonstrates, there are many options when it comes to self-distribution. The environment is constantly changing as technological innovations continue to democratize distribution, creating opportunities for bold independent filmmakers.

What about traditional distribution?

We strongly advocate for self-distribution, but the squad can pivot to a hybrid or traditional distribution strategy if they're aware of the risks and rewards.

Traditional Distribution
Selling a film to a distributor who releases the film to audiences by licensing it through third-party companies. The film's producers get their revenue from royalty fees and/or an advance "minimum guarantee" payment from the distributor. Distributors often have worldwide rights and marketing control, but can leverage exclusive sales channels to reach a wide audience.

A benefit of using the Lean Filmmaking method is leveraging an engaged community of fans to negotiate better terms with a traditional distributor.

And if the film is produced on a tight budget, a low minimum guarantee could cover costs or even make a small profit.

Distributors may even come to you if the film has already demonstrated success on a platform, like being in the top ten on the iTunes charts. SVODs tend to acquire films in a popular genre or niche that's already performing well on their platforms.

Major distributors also have access to channels that are almost impossible for independent filmmakers to leverage, like cinema exhibitors, airlines, hotel chains, cable and free-to-air TV networks, giving the film a much wider audience.

The downside is that it can take a long time to execute a traditional distribution strategy, as industry-agreed release windows ensure each channel has exclusivity for a set time period – though these windows are constantly being challenged by the ever-changing environment and consumer demand.

It can also take a long time to see any royalties (if ever).

But there's still a lot of prestige associated with traditional distribution which may be more important to the squad than making money.

And the good news is that once the deal is done, you don't have to spend more time on distribution. The squad can happily move on to their next project.

Run marketing and sales experiments

The squad can run sales and marketing experiments to explore the best distribution channels for their fans, creating opportunities to launch the film through testing and learning.

This work is done simultaneously, as the most appropriate marketing campaigns are often determined by the chosen sales channel.

You've got the marketing basics covered: a polished trailer, poster and fan email list.

If you haven't already, now's the time to finalize the film title, secure social media handles, create a media kit, purchase a domain and build a simple website with an opt-in to continue growing the fan email list.

There are lots of fantastic free marketing apps, tools and platforms, but it's easy to underestimate the amount of time and energy it takes to manage campaigns.

Don't fall into the trap of trying to do everything – instead, focus on the places and platforms most important to your fans.

The squad does this by running marketing and sales experiments.

To run an experiment:
- Formulate hypothesis to test
- Plan the work
- Do the work
- Assess results
- Adjust
- Repeat

In this step, fan feedback comes from analytics, conversion rates and sales data, rather than interviews.

The squad can use some of the ceremonies practiced in earlier cycles, but apply them to running experiments.

For example, the squad can formulate the test during cycle planning, use standups to facilitate open communication while doing the work, and hold a squad retrospective to discuss the results.

Below are some different examples of experiments:
- Test pricing levels – what are fans willing to pay? Can you make fewer sales at a higher price point for greater overall profit? Is there a freemium model?
- Test lead generators on social media, converting engagement (likes, comments, shares, saves) to an email opt-in
- Test Facebook ads to improve the click-through rate (CTR) and reduce the cost to acquire paying fans
- Test which media outlets are interested in your film by pitching stories to different editors or publishers

- Test which social media platforms work best to convert trailer views to film purchase
- Test segments of the fanbase for their response to different marketing messages or sales platforms
- Test the copy on your website, email headings and social media posts to find the call-to-action (CTA) that consistently resonates with your fans

Focus on running experiments with the biggest potential impact, that can be quickly tested and easily put into action.

Release the film

Like everything else in Lean Filmmaking, the traditional notions of releasing a film are challenged.

By using the Lean Filmmaking method, the squad has essentially been launching versions of the film in every step.

Even in this final step there are multiple soft launches to validate the sales channels and test the marketing campaigns, rather than one big all-or-nothing launch.

After the squad launches on their preferred distribution channel(s), and can consistently sell the film to fans, they can focus their efforts on releasing in different territories and more platforms. The goal is finding an acquisition pipeline that reliably attracts fans who consistently purchase the film.

But it may still be worthwhile to host launch events.

These events are an excellent way to build community and reward those people who've supported the film.

Launches can also be used for publicity, especially if they're designed as aspirational events for specialist media outlets and influencers relevant to fans.

It's also a great time for the squad to celebrate!

Even if the squad decides against a "proper" launch, take a moment to appreciate how far you've come – it's a huge achievement to complete an independent feature film.

In our hypothetical example for *Solo Woman Traveler*, the squad did weekly sales and marketing experiments.

Our squad did a pre-sale crowdfunding campaign to raise the additional cash needed to market and distribute the film. The rewards included exclusive early-bird access to the film and invitations to launch parties. We successfully reached our goal of $7,500 with the support of 250 fans.

This cash was used for the website build, email service provider, paid digital advertising, launch event costs, Digital Cinema Package (DCP) mastering, closed captioning and OTT fees.

We grew our email list to 2,000 subscribers and used paid digital advertising to sign up 200 new subscribers every month. Our conversion rate from email subscriber to film customer was 4%. This was initially a small number of sales but added up to over $3,000 in the first year with minimal effort by using automated processes and evergreen content.

We sold the film directly to our fans through an OTT service provider for more control, optimization and sales analysis. We tested different pricing levels to increase the average spend per customer and added merchandise like branded koozies, travel accessories and apparel.

We sold a movie night package directly to hostels and travel groups with instructions and marketing assets to help make their events a success. Every month the squad contacted at least forty prospects with a close rate of 30%. We charged $100 for this package, which added up to over $14,000 annually.

We made a deal with a major hostel chain for distribution worldwide through their locations, negotiating a one-off fee of $50,000. This allowed us to pay back our initial investment and all of the squad's outstanding deferred fees.

After six months of consistent film sales, we looked for joint ventures to further expand the universe we'd created. We collaborated with a talented artist to produce several graphic novels, partnered with a travel brand on a line of backpacks and started planning a sequel!

It's out, now what?

After the film is released, there'll hopefully come a time when it doesn't take much effort to market the film and sales are easily generated.

Despite this, there's still some ongoing or ad-hoc post-launch management.

Before the squad disbands, or moves onto a new project, here are some final considerations to resolve:
- × If the film is financially successful, it will have a long tail of sales for years to come. How will the revenue be managed and distributed to squad members?
- × The fan database and email list are important assets that can be used again for films with similar themes or subject matter. Who's responsible for maintaining the list and communicating regularly?
- × If ongoing film sales are dependent on paid digital advertising or consistent social media posting, who's in charge of producing this content?
- × What are the expectations for responding to any enquiries from fans, collaborators, distributors or media?

Finally, running one final squad retrospective will help everyone understand what to improve for the next project.

If the squad has ambitions to work together in the future, it would be useful to document the key learnings from making this film.

You're really done when...

You've launched an independent feature film into the market.

You've built a community of fans based on trust and credibility that's been cultivated over time.

You've developed a self-distribution strategy with validated marketing campaigns to consistently attract fans and deliver sales with little time, money or energy.

You've decided there's a diminishing return on investment and the effort required no longer justifies any more work on the film.

The squad has successfully achieved its goals.

That's it. The film is officially done. Woo-hoo!

Step 5 Checklist

- × Run marketing and sales experiments
- × Create marketing assets
- × Secure distribution channel(s)
- × Initiate marketing campaigns
- × Host launch events (and celebrate!)
- × Decide post-launch management strategy
- × Document key learnings

Conclusion

We've distilled everything we've learned so far into this book to ignite your creativity and motivate you to take action.

We hope that creating an independent feature film now feels like it's within your reach.

The best way to truly understand Lean Filmmaking is to put it into practice on a real project.

You don't need to know everything before you start.

Just start where you are. Learn by doing!

We encourage you to embrace the mystery of discovery, pursue experimentation, cultivate curiosity and celebrate inventiveness.

As you become an expert in the Lean Filmmaking method, you'll streamline techniques and adapt tools for your own needs, developing your own cadence. When the philosophy becomes second nature, the squad can concentrate even more on the creative elements of filmmaking.

As you embark on your creative filmmaking journey, remember...

There's a time for learning, reading, thinking and talking, but ultimately the real impact comes from doing. Filmmakers *make* films.

We can't wait to see your unique ideas come to life.

Together, let's change the future of independent filmmaking.

Glossary

Affinity Mapping

A practical and powerful tool that quickly generates ideas, sparks insights and uncovers thematic patterns, captured on sticky notes. It can be used in a variety of circumstances, including creating goals and exploring story concepts.

Ceremonies

Important events during the standard MSA Cycle that facilitate the successful delivery of a full film, either a draft or polish. Ceremonies empower the squad by reinforcing collaboration, strengthening communication and continuously improving the squad's workflow. All squad members participate in these ceremonies.

There are four ceremonies in each cycle: cycle planning, standups, fan experience improvement review and squad retrospective.

Coffee Convo

A type of tester video that's an acted scenario where two friends have watched an imaginary film and they're chatting over coffee about how it made them feel, as if it's a real film. It needs two actors and a smartphone, and can be shot in one take with the actors improvising the conversation (or performing a script).

Core Value: Collaboration is key

We prioritize working together in ways that strengthen meaningful collaboration.

This is achieved by operating in small squads that are cross-functional, non-hierarchical and self-organizing, with everyone sharing responsibility for delivering the film.

Core Value: Fan focused first

We challenge the squad to see their film through the eyes of their fans, from inception to completion, for a compelling fan experience.

This is achieved by forging enduring connections with fans through ongoing research, interviews and practical tools so feedback can be timely and relevant.

Core Value: Learn by doing

We believe there's no substitute for hands-on learning experiences. The squad actively gains insights by doing the work, rather than wasting time on excessive documentation and arbitrary planning.

This is achieved by embedding continuous learning into the process, providing regular opportunities for the squad to adjust their ideas based on outcomes and shifting away from perfection towards experimentation.

Core Value: Story before production values

We believe that powerful storytelling is intrinsic to the merit of films. Our creative effort is focused on validating the story first, then enhancing the film by adding production values.

This is achieved by delivering a version of the full film rather than a formal script, testing assumptions through iterative Make-Show-Adjust Cycles and deferring investment in production values until the story has proven its appeal to fans.

Cycle Planning

A ceremony held at the beginning of the Make stage. The squad commits to the amount of work as an achievable goal for the cycle. The squad chooses the appropriate number of fan experience improvements to be executed in the cycle and breaks them into individual tasks.

Fan

A person willing to invest their time, attention and money in a film. They're the ideal customer who will buy, watch and recommend the film. The squad gathers knowledge about these fans: their feelings, motivations and preferred means of communication.

Fan Experience

The emotions people feel while watching the film and how they describe the story after it's over. The squad's aim is to test, validate and improve the viewing experience until it connects deeply with the intended fans.

Fan Experience Improvements

Incremental changes, executed in MSA Cycles, to test if the fan experience can be improved by their inclusion. They are self-contained, verifiable and small enough to be completed in one cycle.

Each individual improvement is written on an index card in a standard way: Improve the film by [insert fan experience improvement] so fans feel [insert emotion].

Fan Experience Improvement Review

A ceremony that happens at the start of the Adjust stage. The squad decides which fan experience improvements succeeded or failed, based on feedback gathered in the cycle. Fan experience improvements are added, removed, adjusted and prioritized on the Story Scaffold backlog.

Fan Review

A type of group feedback session facilitated by the squad after fan screenings. Most commonly, fans answer three questions about the film: what was your favorite part, how did it make you feel, and what was confusing.

Fan Screening: Free

The squad invites fans to a free event, either for an in-person live screening or online viewing experience, then gets feedback through interviews and/or surveys. The goal is for the squad to test that the story is connecting with the intended fan experience.

Fan Screening: Paid

The squad invites fans to purchase tickets, either for an in-person live screening or online viewing experience, then gets feedback through interviews and/or surveys. The goal is for the squad to test the market viability of their film with fans.

Filmmakathon

A weekend event loosely based on the structure of a tech hackathon, specifically designed for filmmakers to learn and practice the fundamentals of Lean Filmmaking. Over a weekend, participants make short films in four MSA Cycles, from nothing to done, culminating in a reverse screening in front of a live audience.

Full-film Drafts

Lo-fi versions of the entire film created in Make-Show-Adjust Cycles, with the aim of continuously improving the story, exploring the fan experience and ultimately finding Story–Fan Fit.

Full-film Polishes

Hi-fi versions of the entire film made in Make-Show-Adjust Cycles, using technical craft skills to apply appropriate production values that deliver the fan experience, ultimately finding Production–Fan Fit.

Go/No Go Meeting

A predetermined time when the squad can frankly assess the pros and cons of the project and decide whether or not to continue work on the film. It's an opportunity for every squad member to honestly share their reasons for proceeding or stopping, while evaluating if it's still worth investing time, energy and resources into the project.

Impact-vs-Difficulty Matrix

A tool to help the squad make informed decisions about prioritizing the impact and difficulty of fan experience improvements. One axis of the matrix represents the level of impact from trivial to essential, and the other axis is the degree of difficulty from moderate to extreme.

Just-in-time Production

Decisions are made as close to the act of doing the work as possible. Instead of deciding every last detail upfront, planning is purposely kept minimal. Ideally, production decisions are delayed until the last responsible time until the investment has been validated by fans.

Lean Filmmaking

A new way to make films with creativity at its heart that enhances collaboration, uses ongoing iterative cycles and forges a deep connection between filmmakers and their fans.

Lean Filmmaking Coach

A person with experience implementing Lean Filmmaking who models the core values and guides the squad through the five-step method. The coach helps to ensure continuous improvement, provides support to squad members and champions the process.

Lean Filmmaking Core Values

The philosophy of Lean Filmmaking combines Make-Show-Adjust Cycles with four core values: collaboration is key, fan focused first, story before production values and learn by doing.

Lean Filmmaking Independent Feature Film Accelerator

A fifteen-week structured program where squads are coached in developing full-film drafts of independent feature films. Designed for filmmakers who have already produced short-form content and are taking the leap into their first feature film.

Lean Filmmaking Method

A five-step unconventional guide to creating independent feature films from development to distribution, using the Lean Filmmaking philosophy.

Step 1: Form Squad – Find creative collaborators with the balanced combination of skills needed to make a film.

Step 2: Discover Fans – Find an idea that deeply resonates with fans and the squad.

Step 3: Develop Drafts – Find a connection between a story worth telling and the fans who want to see it by running MSA Cycles.

Step 4: Produce Polishes – Find the connection between a well-crafted film and the fans who want to buy it by running MSA Cycles.

Step 5: Launch Film – Find distribution channels and marketing campaigns that consistently make sales for the squad.

Make-Show-Adjust Cycles

The work of planning, filming and learning is organized into small continuous cycles. Squads use basic cycles to produce tester videos, then standard cycles for full-film drafts and polishes, before ultimately converging on the final version of the film.

The main difference (apart from the length) between a basic cycle used to make tester videos and a standard Make-Show-Adjust Cycle is the inclusion of formal ceremonies.

The Make stage includes all the work required to complete a version of a tester video or the full film, the Show stage screens this to fans and the Adjust stage uses fan feedback and squad learnings to decide improvements for the next cycle.

Overlapping Activities

Restructuring the work involved in making a film to overlap, instead of being completed in a linear fashion. This is a collaborative way to improve output and efficiently distribute the workload between squad members.

Production–Fan Fit

A strong connection between a well-crafted film and the fans who want to purchase it. This is achieved by using Make-Show-Adjust Cycles to produce full-film polishes that validate production values with fans.

Project Success Target

The intersection of the creative ambitions of the squad, their constraints and the interest from fans. The best opportunities for a successful film project target this crossover.

Reaction Interview

In-person conversations with fans conducted by the squad after showing tester videos or the full film, to gauge the fan experience and ascertain if the hypothesis being tested has succeeded or failed.

Research Interview

In-person conversations with fans conducted by the squad before drafting a fan experience, to investigate the spark of an idea and understand the worldview of potential fans.

Self-distribution

Selling a film directly to fans, rather than selling it to a distributor. The film's producers get their revenue from their customers. It's labor-intensive but there's a capacity to earn a higher percentage of the profits and retain creative control.

Squad

A group of three to nine multi-skilled people with the combined experience to make a film, including writing, directing, acting, editing, shooting, producing and marketing. Everyone is involved for the duration of making the film, from development to distribution. The overarching purpose of each squad member is to successfully deliver a film to fans, not just execute their specific role.

Squad Retrospective

A ceremony held at the end of the Adjust stage. The squad reflects on their workflow, making improvements for future cycles. Most commonly, everyone answers three questions about the cycle: what worked, what didn't work, and what was confusing.

Standups

Ceremonies that happen during the Make stage when the squad meets for quick status updates. They're short catch-ups to communicate which tasks each squad member is doing and troubleshoot issues that may hinder the completion of the work.

Story–Fan Fit

A strong connection between a story worth telling and the fans who want to see it. This is achieved by using Make-Show-Adjust Cycles to develop full-film drafts that validate the story with fans.

Story Scaffold

An ephemeral physical or digital representation, illustrating the current version of the entire story and assisting the squad in visualizing the film's structure to achieve the desired fan experience.

Tester Video

Any kind of lo-fi video content used to validate the fan experience. It's short, easy to produce and has a specific hypothesis to test with fans.

Traditional Distribution

Selling a film to a distributor who releases the film to audiences by licensing it through third-party companies. The film's producers get their revenue from royalty fees and/or an advance "minimum guarantee" payment from the distributor. Distributors often have worldwide rights and marketing control, but can leverage exclusive sales channels to reach a wide audience.

About Lean Filmmaking

Lean Filmmaking was founded by cheeky provocateurs, creative agitators and siblings Kylie Eddy and David Eddy.

They combined their filmmaking experience and agile expertise to re-imagine the development, production and distribution of independent films for an uncertain world.

Their goal is to empower filmmakers to create independent feature films using the Lean Filmmaking method.

They celebrate experimentation and inventiveness, and help filmmakers to forge a sustainable artistic practice.

Their mission is to make filmmaking accessible to everyone – especially underrepresented people – and enable more diverse storytelling on the screen.

To share your experiences in applying the Lean Filmmaking method, email book@leanfilmmaking.com.

This book is only the beginning!

Go to leanfilmmaking.com and become part of the movement to transform independent filmmaking.

Kylie and David are available for speaking opportunities, coaching and workshop facilitation. They also produce events that are challenging, mind-bending and designed to blast through creative blocks.

For more information about bookings or bulk book sales, email kylie@leanfilmmaking.com.

Acknowledgments

To our Lean Filmmaking community – if you've ever attended a meetup, read our early blog, participated in a Filmmakathon or joined a squad, this book is for you. Thank you for believing in us.

There've been countless supporters who have contributed to our development over the years and we've loved all of the spirited conversations and mind-blowing moments. Thanks to the many people who've been important sounding boards at crucial times, including Beth Biederman, Mekelle Mills, Sarah Harney, Emma Gibson, Edwina Exton, Simon Britton, Chris Mander, Simon J Green, Bo Wen Xi, Josh Janssen, Amber Harris, Chris Kamen, Alessandro Frosali...and especially Chelsea Denny, who deserves some kind of award for being part of every experiment we've ever run.

To the participants of the inaugural Independent Feature Film Accelerator who helped test the method: Paul Anthony Nelson, Perri Cummings, Ric Forster and Melanie Rowland. Being first takes a massive leap of faith; thank you for trusting us. Your creativity, tenacity and talent is inspiring. What we learned from you has become the foundation of so many concepts in this book.

We'd like to thank everyone who generously shared their practical, thoughtful and honest feedback on early drafts, including Brenda Leeuwenberg, Oliver Staton, Daphane Ng, Lee-Ann Woon, Marie Kelly, Dr Jen Frahm and Lena Ross.

And to the first one hundred readers who followed us on LeanPub as we did iterations of the book, just knowing you were out there helped motivate us to keep going.

Finally, to our wonderful editor, Irene Kalpakas. We're grateful for your tireless commitment that has made this book better than we ever could have imagined. Your guidance, encouragement and friendship means the world to us.

Kylie thanks: The amazing people in my life who accept me no matter what and make everything better – Tamsin Gatewood, Mitzi Zagon, Rachel Bailey, Conrad Browne, Clinton Bermingham and Paul Tonta.

David thanks: My wife Dominik, who's been part of the journey (supporting, reviewing and helping), and my kids who show me how exciting everything is.

We both thank our parents Denise and Robert, who always said we could achieve anything we put our minds to. We love you.

www.ingramcontent.com/pod-product-compliance
Lightning Source LLC
Chambersburg PA
CBHW071959290426
44109CB00018B/2069